QUESTIONS EVERY JEHOVAH'S WITNESS SHOULD BE ASKED

A penetrating examination of the
Errors and Evils of the Watchtower

IAN BROWN

AMBASSADOR
EMERALD INTERNATIONAL

GREENVILLE, SOUTH CAROLINA • BELFAST, NORTHERN IRELAND

Sixty Questions Every Jehovah's Witness
Should be Asked
© 2002 Ian Brown
Printed in Canada

Ambassador Emerald International
427 Wade Hampton Boulevard
Greenville, S.C. 29609 U.S.A.

and

Ambassador Productions Ltd.
Providence House
Ardenlee Street
Belfast BT6 8QJ, Northern Ireland

www.emeraldhouse.com

cover design and page layout by A & E Media,
Sam Laterza

ISBN 1 889893 86 2

CONTENTS

Acknowledgments

Special thanks is due to the indomitable Colin Maxwell, whose infectious enthusiasm was the spark that ignited the idea for this book and whose tireless research sent me in the direction of much of the information contained within it; also to Esther Mackey, who left no stone unturned as she performed the rather unenviable task of not only proofreading the book, but checking every Bible reference in it.

Abbreviations

(NWT) . . . . .New World Translation of the Holy Scriptures. This translation of the Bible was produced by Jehovah's Witnesses and contains numerous changes in the wording of key passages that reflect the interpretations of the group's leaders.

(KJV) . . . . .King James Version of the Scriptures

(WTS / WBTS) . .Watch Tower Bible & Tract Society

(WT) . . . . .Watch Tower Magazine

(ZWTR) . . . . . . .Zion's Watch Tower Reprints

(JWs) . . . . .Jehovah's Witnesses

(Gr) . . . . .Greek

INTRODUCTION

Many people are of the opinion that those who call themselves Jehovah's Witnesses are real "authorities" on the Bible. To any average outsider they certainly give the impression of knowing their Bibles and of having an apparent biblical answer to every question floated in their direction. One of their standard advertisements, inviting people to their meetings, announces:

KNOW YOUR BIBLE
IT CAN BE AN OPEN BOOK TO YOU.
FREE BIBLE COURSES EACH WEEK.

Appearances, however, may be deceptive. This is one instance when they *most definitely are*. Jehovah's Witnesses are NOT Bible students in the truest sense of that term, and the Bible is most certainly NOT an open book to them.

For one thing, they have insufficient free time to conduct any detailed personal study of the Scriptures. A typical week for a Jehovah's Witness will involve the following:

1. Prepare, by underlining, the answers to the "Watchtower" study.
2. Prepare, by reading, the material set for the tour talks in the ministry school.
3. Prepare the material from "Our Kingdom Ministry" for the service meeting.
4. Prepare, by underlining, the material for the house group study.
5. Ten to fifteen minutes daily Bible reading.

6. Read each day's text and comments drawn from the "Watchtower" magazine.
7. Spend time preparing for interested persons.

In addition, the Jehovah's Witness is required to:

8. Conduct a family study each week.
9. Spend two and a half hours weekly in door-to-door work.
10. Read the four thirty-two-paged magazines produced each month.
11. Keep up with the latest Watchtower booklets, tracts and books.
12. Prepare for, and study with, outsiders.
13. Prepare any talk assignment.
14. Attend all five meetings each week.

Also, the organization to which they belong, while giving the impression that it encourages deep personal Bible study, actually discourages it. With typical craft, the WBTS suggests that because the Jehovah's Witnesses are limited in their free time:

"We may think of study as hard work, as involving heavy research. But in Jehovah's organization it is not necessary to spend a lot of time and energy in research, for there are brothers in the organization who are assigned to do that very thing, to help you who do not have so much time for this, these preparing the good material in The Watchtower and other publications of the Society." [WT, 1 June 1967, p. 338].

The majority of time spent in study by Jehovah's Witnesses is based around Watchtower material that is careful to present the Bible the watchtower way. Official teaching is, that without the organization, no one can arrive at a proper understanding of Scripture; individuals cannot interpret the Bible.

The following quotations from the *Watchtower* magazine reveal the degree of authority the Watchtower organization aims to exert over the minds of its members:

"Jehovah God caused the Bible to be written in such a way that one needs to come in touch with His human channel before one can fully and accurately understand it. True, we need the help of God's Holy Spirit, but its help also comes to us primarily by association with the channel Jehovah God sees fit to use." [WT, 15 February 1981, p. 17].

"Jehovah's organization alone, in all the earth, is directed by God's Holy Spirit or active force (Zechariah 4:6). Only this organization functions for Jehovah's purpose and to His praise. To it alone God's Sacred Word, the Bible, is not a sealed book." [WT, 1 July 1973, p. 402].

"Fight against independent thinking.... If we get to thinking that we know better than the organization, we should ask ourselves: "Where did we learn Bible truth in the first place? Would we know the way of the truth if it had not been for guidance from the organization? Really, can we get along without the direction of God's organization?" No we cannot." [WT, l5 January 1983, p. 27].

Jehovah's Witnesses give total allegiance to the dictates of an organization and allow that organization to interpret the Scriptures for them. However, as the questions and facts contained in this book demonstrate, that organization is very far removed from the plain teachings of God's Holy Scripture, and, instead of opening the Bible to the minds of its adherents, it actually obscures God's Word by manipulating, misrepresenting and denying its truth.

All verses quoted in the course of the sixty questions in this book are taken from the New World Translation (NWT)* —a version which I neither endorse nor recommend, but, because the Jehovah's Witnesses are taught to trust no other version, I believe it best to expose the fallacies of their organization and beliefs using their own materials (cf. p. 84).

If the Watchtower decides to change any of these verses (as they have done with Hebrews 1:6 and other scriptures), then the obvious question for the individual Jehovah's Witness is, "Why did the WBTS change their own Bible?"

NOTE: unless otherwise indicated the NWT quotations, which appear in this book, are from the1961 edition.

I have written this book in question form as a result of some advice from former Jehovah's Witnesses who know (only too well) how difficult it is to penetrate the mind control imposed on the individual by the Watchtower organization. They have taught me that, instead of opting for the confrontational route and arguing against the JW in an effort to win him for Christ, it is better to ask questions.

No doubt many who read this book will have engaged a JW in disputes over doctrine on the doorstep. You will have quoted a verse of Scripture, only for the JW to counter that with another verse (he is taught to respond with something, whether it is relevant or not). The net result of such debate is usually frustration and exasperation.

To ask questions takes advantage of the JW's programming. As they are programmed to run away from someone who is trying to free them from the Watchtower, so they are also persuaded to believe that they are the *only ones* who can really help you and answer your questions. If you ask a JW, "Please help me with my questions," he is going to want to stay around and do just that; however, if your introductory line is, "Look, here's what's wrong with the Watchtower" he will quickly disappear, labeling you (as he has been taught) an agent of the devil.

Say to the JW that you have taken some interest in the organization he belongs to and have done a little research on it... "Could you help me with a few questions I have?" That will trigger the programmed response.

Always keep this truth in mind: in spite of the authoritative air expressed by the JWs when they come to your doorstep, you may be 100% assured that there are sound Biblical answers for all of the Jehovah's Witness errors, and there is a multitude of questions with which they cannot cope.

If this little book helps God's people in countering the falsehoods of the Watchtower Society, or serves to send a ray of gospel light into some Jehovah's Witness' darkness, I will feel richly rewarded for the time spent in producing it, and my ultimate aim will be achieved: the Lord, Jehovah, will be glorified.

Ian Brown
Londonderry

* The New World Translation of the Holy Scriptures" is a version of the Bible produced by Jehovah's Witnesses themselves. It was completed in portions from 1950 to 1960, with the complete Bible revised and issued in 1961. Their Bible has been revised several times since then in 1970, 1971, 1981 and 1984. Many Biblical scholars have examined this "translation" and have found it to contain many errors, plus numerous changes in the wording of key passages (totally unsupported by the original Hebrew and Greek texts of the Scriptures) that reflect the interpretations and promote the doctrines of the Watchtower.

SOURCE OF AUTHORITY

Although the JW will say that the Bible is his authority, it is clear that the Watchtower publications take precedence over the Bible; these are his primary source of authority.

When the JWs use the Bible, they refer to their own version —the "New World Translation" (NWT). This translation contains numerous unwarranted changes in the wording of key passages that reflect the interpretations of the group's leaders. Therefore, how the leaders interpret the Bible—and NOT the Bible itself—is the final authority for the JWs. [cf. "Quote To Note," pp. 10–13].

C.T. Russell, founder of the WTS, called himself "God's mouthpiece" and claimed that compared to reading his books, Bible reading is "a waste of time." [WT, 15 July 1906, p. 229; 15 September 1910, p. 298]

Allegiance to Watchtower Teaching

1. According to the WBTS, all Jehovah's Witnesses "must adhere absolutely to the decisions and scriptural understanding of the Society because God has given it authority over his people" [WT 1 May 1972, p. 272] What is the Scriptural basis for a Christian giving absolute adherence to a fallible organization?

2. The WBTS urges, "Avoid independent thinking... questioning the counsel that is provided by God's visible organization" [WT 15 January 1983, pp. 22–27], thus locking its adherents into the interpretation the Watchtower organization places on the Bible. Should we not rather follow the procedure Paul laid down *under divine revelation...* "test the inspired expressions to see whether they originated with God" (1 John 4:1), and:

"I speak as to men with discernment; judge for yourselves what I say" (1 Corinthians 10:15). Surely these Scriptures also oblige us to examine the teachings of the Watchtower Society independently.

3. Why do the JWs persist in quoting Proverbs 4:18–"But the path of the righteous ones is like the bright light that is getting lighter and lighter until the day is firmly established," as cover for the multitude of failed prophecies and doctrinal somersaults over the course of their history, since the context of this text determines that Proverbs 4:18 is contrasting the enlightened path of the righteous with the darkened path of the wicked (cf. vs.14, 19)? It does NOT mean that the righteous stumble in the wrong direction until they receive "new light" to set them straight.

NOTE: If "new truths" contradict old teachings, then the "old light" must actually have been darkness.

When the Watchtower sect was still in its infancy, founder Charles Taze Russell castigated the practice of using "the light-getting-brighter doctrine" as an excuse for failed predictions as one of the flaws of the Adventist sect he left behind.

He declared, "If we were following a man, undoubtedly it would be different with us; undoubtedly one human idea would contradict another and that which was light one or two or six years ago would be regarded as darkness now. But with God there is no variableness, neither shadow of turning, and so it is with truth; any knowledge or light coming from God must be like its author. A new view of truth never can contradict a former truth. "New light" never extinguishes older "light," but adds to it." [Zion's Watch Tower, February 1881, p. 3]

However, as time has gone on, the organization which Russell founded is now doing what he lambasted Adventist movements for doing in the past—introducing "new truths" that contradict former teachings.

"Quote" to Note

George Orwell coined the phrase "double-think" in his futuristic novel *Nineteen Eighty-Four*. JWs appear to have taken this concept to heart, as they insist that their teachings come directly from the Bible, and the Bible alone, while at the same time knowing in their hearts that everything depends on the current interpretation coming from Brooklyn headquarters.

Consider the following series of presumptuous statements which appeared in the *Watchtower* magazine from 1910 to 1981. Each quote demonstrates how the Watchtower Society demands that the Scriptures should only be studied through the "interpretative spectacles" of the Watchtower publications.

1910

"Furthermore, not only do we find that people cannot see the divine plan in studying the Bible by itself, but we see, also, that if any-one lays the "Scripture Studies" (Russell's writings) aside, even after he has used them, after he has read them for ten years... if he then lays them aside and ignores them and goes to the Bible alone, though he has under-stood his Bible for ten years, our experience shows that within two years he goes into darkness.

"On the other hand, if he had merely read the Scripture Studies with their references, and had not read a page of the Bible, as such, he would be in the light at the end of two years, because he would have the light of the Scriptures." [WT, 15 September 1910, p. 298]

1941

"Receiving the gift, (Rutherford's book, *Children*) the marching children clasped it to them, not a toy or plaything for idle pleasure, but the Lord's provided instrument for most effective work in the remaining months before Armageddon." [WT, 15 September 1941, p. 288]

1957

"Jehovah God has provided His holy written word for all mankind and it contains all the information that is needed for men in taking a course leading to life. But God has not arranged for that word to speak independently, or to shine forth life-giving truths by itself. It is through his organization that God provides this light that the prophet says is the teaching or law of the mother. If we walk in the light of truth, we must recognize not only Jehovah God as our father, but his organization as our Mother." [WT, 1 May 1957, p. 273]

1961

"He wants his earthly servants united, and so he has made understanding the Bible today dependent upon associating with his organization." [WT, 1 November 1961, p. 668]

1964

"The Brother went down before breakfast, and when we had breakfast he said, 'Brother Reimer, I got a new *Watchtower* this morning, and do you know the first thing that Ma and I do when we get that Tower? We kneel down before we take the wrapper off and ask Jehovah to make us worthy to see what the message is that Jehovah has for us. Now, before we take the wrapper off, will you kneel down and pray with us?'

How different that elective elder was from this humble couple who appreciated Jehovah's organization." [WT, 15 September 1964]

1965

"He [God] does not impart his holy spirit and an understanding and appreciation of his Word apart from his visible organization." [WT, 1 July 1965, p. 391]

1967

"Thus the Bible is an organizational book and belongs to the Christian congregation as an organization, not to individuals, regardless of how sincerely they may believe that they can interpret the Bible. For this reason the Bible CANNOT be properly understood without Jehovah's visible organization in mind." [WT, 1 October 1967, p. 587]

1981

"...Jehovah God has also provided his visible organization, his "faithful and discreet slave," made up of spirit-anointed ones, to help Christians in all nations to understand and apply properly the Bible in their lives. Unless we are in touch with this channel of communication that God is using, we will not progress along the road of life, no matter how much Bible reading we do." [WT, 1 December 1981, p. 27]

All of this advice from the Watchtower Society runs entirely contrary to the Word of God. It is perfectly obvious that the JWs believe that the writings of Russell and Rutherford take precedence over the Bible.

The New World Translation

Even when the JWs use the Bible, they refer to their own translation—the "New World Translation" (NWT). This version contains numerous changes in the wording of key passages that reflect the interpretations of the group's leaders. Therefore, once again, how the leaders interpret the Bible—and not the Bible itself—emerges as the final authority for the JWs.

In an article entitled "The Word with a Twist," John Whaley states:

"One of the common threads which runs through all of the cults is the twisting of Scripture. Whereas most cults twist the Word of God by quoting the Word inaccurately or by reinterpreting the Word by ignoring the immediate context, there are a few who simply re-translate the Scriptures to fit their preconceived teachings.

"One of the best examples of this practice is found in the New World Translation published by the Watchtower Bible and Tract Society."

There is no doubt about that.

The "New World Translation of the Holy Scriptures," commenced in 1950 and completed by 1960, was produced by a five-man "Translation Committee": N. H. Knorr, F.W. Franz, A. D. Schroeder, G. D. Gangas and M. Henschel.

Consider the following facts about the composition and conduct of that Committee:

(1) The men who comprised the Translation Committee had no adequate schooling or background to function as skilled critical Bible translators.

Apart from Frederick Franz, NONE of the Translation Committee members knew Biblical Greek or Hebrew, and Franz's ability is open to serious question. Franz's "expertise" in the biblical languages amounted to a mere two years of Greek at a university—he was self-taught in Hebrew: yet he was regarded as *the best* Bible translator the Society had.

"Fact" to Track...

Exposure of translator's lack of knowledge in Hebrew. In the Scottish Court Sessions in November, 1954 (just four years after the release of the first part of the Watchtower Scriptures), Frederick Franz answered the attorney as follows under oath:

Q. Have you also made yourself familiar with Hebrew?

A. Yes.

Q. So that you have a substantial linguistic apparatus at your command?

A. Yes, for use in my biblical work.

Q. You, yourself, read and speak Hebrew, do you?

A. I do not speak Hebrew.

Q. You do not?

A. No.

Q. Can you, yourself, translate that into Hebrew?

A. Which?

Q. The fourth verse of the second chapter of Genesis.

A. You mean here?

Q. Yes.

A. No, 1 wouldn't attempt to do that.
["Purser's Proof", pp. 6–7, 102–103]

Russell also deficient in knowledge of Biblical languages. In a libel case, the founder of the Watch Tower and Bible Society, Charles Taze Russell, was questioned about his scholastic standing and admitted that he had left school at fourteen after attending only seven years. He was then questioned about his knowledge of the Greek alphabet and, after supplying some extremely hesitant answers, was asked, "Are you familiar with the Greek language?" to which he answered, "No."

Without the needed proficiency in the original languages, men like Russell, Franz, etc., clearly were not qualified to make a complete —and professedly superior—translation of the entire Scriptures.

Given this lack of ability with the original languages, is it any wonder that:

(2) The Translation Committee Invented non-existent rules of Greek grammar and then proceeded to follow these rules only when necessary to support their peculiar theology.

A clear example of this is John 1:1, where the Translation Committee has rendered the Greek "and the Word was a god." [cf. p. 26]

(3) The Translation Committee made up a Greek tense that is non-existent.

The 1950 edition of their "New World Translation of the Christian Greek Scriptures" rendered the εγω ειμι (ego eimi, "I am") of

John 8:58 as "I have been" and stated that it is "properly rendered in the perfect indefinite tense" in the Greek language. The problem is, there is NOT—and NEVER has been—any "perfect indefinite tense" in *any* language.

After the Watchtower Society was informed of this fact, they made the change to the "perfect tense indicative," but as the Greek student will recognize, this phrase is in the present tense and is correctly translated, "I AM" (cf. Exodus 3:14).

(4) They have added words to Scripture which change the meaning of the texts to agree with their theology.

One need only examine the NWT renderings of John 15:4–5, John 17:26, Galatians 1:16, Romans 8:10, Colossians 1:27 and 2 Corinthians 13:5 to find that the translation committee has paraphrased Scripture to deny the indwelling of Christ in the believer.

Each of the aforementioned verses speaks of Christ living within the Christian ("in him" or "in you"), yet these verses found in the NWT have been paraphrased to read "in union with you (him)."

Other examples include: 2 Peter 1:1 (Question 13, p. 27); Colossians 1:15–17 (Question 20, p. 30); Philippians 2:9 (Question 20, p. 30).

Not Recommended

It is fair to lay the charge that the theology set out in this translation is nothing less than a fatal distortion of Biblical truth.

The Scriptures and the Holy Spirit

The Holy Spirit, through the pen of Paul, requires us to study in order to be "approved unto God, a workman that needeth not to be ashamed, rightly dividing the word of truth" (2 Timothy 2:15, KJV).

That same Holy Spirit illuminates our minds with respect to the truth of God's revealed Word (cf. I Corinthians 2:12–16; 2 Corinthians 3:14–17; Hebrews 9:8; 1 John 2:20, 27; John 14:26; 16:13–15)—we do not need an organization such as the Watchtower to tell us what the Bible says. All we need to do is read, meditate on, and pray over the Scriptures for ourselves and allow the Holy Spirit to give us understanding.

THE TRINITY

The JWs emphatically deny the biblical teaching of the Trinity, caricaturing the Christian belief in the Trinity as pagan.

They believe that God is only the "Jehovah God" referred to in the Old Testament; they deny the concept of one God who exists in three distinct persons—Father, Son and Holy Spirit, claiming that this is a belief in three gods, which is polytheism.

"Satan is the originator of the 'trinity' doctrine," they allege in *Let God Be True*, p. 82.

In the Watchtower's infamous assault on the doctrine of the Trinity, *Should You Believe In the Trinity,* many of the "quotes" are actually misquotes or have been taken out of context.

The Trinity

4. How can the Watchtower Society construe belief in the Trinity (God the Father, God the Son and God the Holy Ghost) as a deception of the devil when:

(i) Genesis 1:26, 3:22 and 11:7 refer to God (Jehovah) in the plural;

(ii) Baptism and benedictions are conferred using "formulae" which identify the three persons in the Trinity (Matthew 28:19, 2 Corinthians 13:14, 1 Peter 1:2);

(iii) Each of these three persons is designated "God" [Greek, Θεος] in Scripture (e.g. The Father, John 6:27; the Son, Hebrews 1:8; the Holy Spirit, Acts 5:3–4).

5. The Jehovah's Witnesses quote Deuteronomy 6:4 as proof that God is not a trinity: "Listen, O Israel: Jehovah our God is ONE Jehovah...." However, why do they insist that the Hebrew word translated "one" in this passage (echad) must refer to an absolute unity only, yet allow that the same word, when it is used in Genesis 2:24 to describe the marriage relationship, must refer to a composite unity: "that is why a man will leave his father and his mother and he must stick to his wife and THEY must become ONE flesh?"

NOTE: Two people = one flesh; therefore, there is no way that the wording of Deuteronomy 6:4 excludes the Trinity; rather, the Hebrew word used for "one" (echad) may well indicate that the reference is to *more than one person*.

6. It is obvious from Zechariah 2:10–12 that Jehovah is the one coming and residing in Jerusalem and that Jehovah of armies has sent Him. How can Jehovah's Witnesses explain this clear case of two persons called Jehovah in the NWT apart from admitting that the only possible answer is that God the Father is sending God the Son?

"Cry out... O daughter of Zion; for here I am coming, and I will reside in the midst of you, is the utterance of Jehovah.... And you will have to know that Jehovah of armies himself has sent me to you. And Jehovah will ... yet choose Jerusalem."

7. When the Scripture is so unequivocal in its teaching that "No one can slave for two masters" (Matthew 6:24), how can James have two separate masters and serve Jesus with the same diligence as Jehovah; James 1:1 "James, a slave of GOD and of the LORD JESUS CHRIST..."?

"Fact" to Track

The first assistant editor of *The Watchtower* (originally *Zion's Watch Tower And Herald Of Christ's Presence*), John H. Paton (Almont, Michigan), was actually a Trinitarian. It was only after Paton left in 1882 that Charles

Russell began to write articles against the Trinity.

"Quote" to **Note**

Deuteronomy 4:31 declares: "For Jehovah your God [God is the plural Hebrew word, Elohim] is a merciful God [God is singular, El]."

A Deceitful Treatment

The Watchtower publication, *Reasoning From The Scriptures* (1985) is often used by JWs to argue their case against the Trinity. The article on the Trinity in *Reasoning* covers some twenty pages (pp. 405–426).

Doug Harris and Bill Browning, writing in their book, *Awake! To The Watch Tower*, have conducted a detailed analysis of *Reasoning's* treatment of the Trinity. They allege that it is characterized by "falseness" and "deception" and point out that the article on the Trinity in *Reasoning*:

(1) Takes selective quotations from various sources and manipulates and twists them to make them say the complete opposite to what their author intended.

(2) Omits to inform its readers that they are using quotes from an anti-Christian group (i.e. the Unitarians, who openly deny both the deity of Christ and the atonement) to try to "prove" their own erroneous doctrines.

Hanis and Browning conclude their analysis of *Reasoning's* article against the Trinity by saying: "How can the WBTS, who call themselves God's channel of truth, twist things so much?"

THE PERSON OF CHRIST

Since they do not recognize the doctrine of the Trinity, the JWs do not accept that Jesus Christ is God, but claim that Jesus is a lesser god.

They claim that the Lord Jesus Christ is the first created being of Jehovah God [*The Kingdom is at Hand*, p46], and attempt to bolster their argument by a mis-translation of Revelation 3:14 and other Scriptures. They also believe that Jesus was the Archangel Michael in heaven [*The Truth Shall Make You Free*, p49], was only a good man who was always inferior to Jehovah God while he was on earth, and was "recreated" by Jehovah as the Archangel Michael in the heavens.

The JWs' Bible [NWT] attempts to remove the Deity of Christ by systematically altering every Biblical passage that teaches it.

The Person of Christ

8. The NWT translates John 1:1 as "...and the Word was with God, and the Word was a god." Since there is no indefinite article ("a") in the Greek text of John 1:1 (and experts in the Greek language maintain that Θεος ην ο Λογος must be rendered as, "The Word was God"), why has the NWT added the word "a" in front of "god" in breach of the rules of Greek grammar?

9. The JWs claim (quoting Deuteronomy 6:4) to worship only one God, Jehovah, while they accuse Trinitarians of being polytheistic for worshipping Christ as God. However, by insisting that John 1:1 should be translated, "The Word was a god," are they not guilty of polytheism, for they are saying that Jesus Christ is one of the gods?

NOTE: In translating John 1:1 the way they do, the JWs display another blatant inconsistency. While they are quick to slip in the indefinite article in John 1:1, in a mischievous effort to back up their own false teaching, why, when the word "God" does not have an article in other verses in the same chapter (vv. 6, 12, 13 and 18), do they NOT bother to supply the indefinite article "a" in ANY of these verses?

"Fact" to Track

Between 1962 and 1983 the WBTS quoted Johannes Greber to support their translation of John 1:1, even though they knew in 1956 that Greber's wife acted as a spirit medium to produce the translation. They no longer quote Greber but it is still interesting to ask the Witnesses why they think their translation agrees with a spiritist Bible and why "God's organization" knowingly used that spiritist Bible as a reliable source for many years.

10. In Matthew 1:23, who does Matthew say has been given the name which means "With Us Is God"?

11. The Bible says that only Jehovah is our Savior (Hosea 13:4, Isaiah 43:11, 45:21, etc.). How then can Jesus Christ be identified as our Savior? (Luke 2:11, Philippians 3:20, Titus 2:13, 3:6, 2 Peter 1:1, 2:20, 3:18, etc.)?

12. "Who can forgive sins except one, God?" (Mark 2:7) is a question every Jehovah's Witness would do well to ponder in the light of the fact that Scripture identifies both Jehovah and Jesus as having the power and authority to forgive sins (cf. Numbers 14:18, Psalm 103:2–3, Isaiah 43:25 and Daniel 9:9 with Matthew 9:2, Luke 24:47, John 1:29 and Acts 10:43).

13. In 2 Peter 1:1, the NWT inserts the word "the." "Simon Peter, a slave and apostle of Jesus Christ, to those who have obtained a faith, held in equal privilege with ours, by the righteousness of our God and [the] Savior Jesus Christ." Why is it inserted? How would the verse read if the word 'the" were NOT inserted? What does Scripture say about adding words to the Bible? (cf. Proverbs 30:5–6).

14. Who is identified as "the first and the last" in Scripture?

- JEHOVAH is referred to as the "first" and the "last" in Isaiah 44:6 and 48:12, and Revelation 21:6, in speaking of GOD, says, "...I am the Alpha and the Omega, the beginning and the end...."
- But in Revelation 22:12–13, Jesus says of himself, "I am the Alpha and the Omega, the first and the last, the beginning and the end." Again, in Revelation 1:17–18, Jesus refers to himself as the first and the last. How can this be since by definition, there can be only one first and last? Is this not conclusive evidence that Christ is Jehovah Jesus?

NOTE: Within a period of two months in 1978, official Watchtower publications said that the "Alpha and Omega" of Revelation refers to:

- (i) Jehovah God (*Awake!* 22 August 1978, p. 28);
- (ii) Jesus Christ (*Watchtower*, 1 October 1978, p. 15).

If only the Watchtower Society were able to add "two and two" together...

15. If Jesus Christ is not Jehovah God, why is He called, "Jehovah is our Righteousness" (Jeremiah 23:5–6; cf. 1 Corinthians 1:30)?

16. Jesus Christ is referred to as "Mighty God" in Isaiah 9:6 ("For there has been a child born to us, there has been a son given to us ... And his name will be called Wonderful Counsellor, Mighty God ..."). Jehovah is referred to as "Mighty God" in Isaiah 10:20–21 and Jeremiah 32:18. How can this be if there is only one God (1 Corinthians 8:4, Isaiah 43:10, 44:6)?

17. If Jesus were formerly known as the Archangel Michael [*The Truth Shall Make You Free*, p. 49; WT, 1 November 1995, p. 81], why does the Bible make it abundantly clear that Michael is a created angel who does not have the authority to rebuke Satan (Jude 9), whereas the Lord Jesus *did* rebuke Satan (Matthew 4:10)?

18. In Luke 4:12, the NWT translates *kurios* (Gr-lord) as "Jehovah," which makes the verse read, "You must not put Jehovah your God to the test." [See Gr-Engl Interlinear]. Why is *kurios* translated as "Jehovah" in this verse? Was the devil, in Luke 4:9–11, putting Jehovah to the test or JESUS to the test?

19. The NWT translates the Greek word *kurios* (Gr—lord) as "Jehovah" more than twenty-five times in the New Testament (Matthew 3:3, Luke 2:9, John 1:23, Acts 21:14, Romans 12:19, Colossians 1:10, 1 Thessalonians 5:2, 1 Peter 1:25, Revelation 4:8, etc.). Why is the word "Jehovah" translated when it does NOT appear in the Greek text? Why is the NWT not consistent in translating *kurios* as "Jehovah" in Romans 10:9, 1 Corinthians 12:3, Philippians 2:11, 2 Thessalonians 2:1 and Revelation 22:21?

Christ and Creation

20. In Colossians 1:15–17, the NWT inserts the word "other" four times even though it is NOT in the original Greek [see Gr-Engl interlinear]. Why is the word "other" inserted? How would these verses read if the word "other" had not been inserted? (Note: The NWT has treated Philippians 2:9 in the same way: the word "other" has been added without warrant).

21. John 1:3 says in reference to Christ, "All things came into existence through him, and apart from him not even one thing came into existence." How could Christ have been a created being if ALL things came into existence through Him? (If Jesus was a created being, then according to John 1:3, Jesus would have had to create himself).

22. If Christ was created by God and was the wisdom of God (Proverbs 8:1–4, 12, 22–31), then before Jesus would have been created, God would have had to have been without wisdom. How is it possible that God could ever have been without wisdom?

23. Why do JWs say that the description of Christ in Revelation 3:14—"the beginning of the creation by God"—means that Jesus was the first to be created by Jehovah when (i) their own Kingdom Interlinear Translation reveals that the Greek *should* be translated "of God," NOT "by God"; and (ii) the Greek word "*archi*" (translated "beginning") means the beginning in the sense of source, i.e. Jesus is the source of all God's creation?

24. Colossians 1:16, in talking about Jesus, says that "... All [other] things have been created through him and for Him." If Jesus were Michael the Archangel at the time of creation, would an angel have created all things for himself? Isaiah 43:7 says Jehovah (the "Creator" and "Former") created "everyone... for my own glory."

25. The NWF translates the Greek words εγω ωιμι as "I am" every time it appears (John 6:35, 6:41, 8:24, 13:19, 15:5, etc.), except in John 8:58 where it is translated: "Before Abraham came into existence, *I have been.*" What is the reason for the inconsistency in this translation? If εγω ωιμι were

translated in John 8:58 the same way it is
translated in every other verse in which it
appears, how would John 8:58 read?

26. The Scriptures tell us in one place that
Jesus raised up His body (John 2:19–22;
10:17–18) and in another place that GOD
raised up His body (Acts 2:24; Romans 10:9).
Since the Bible does not contradict itself,
what does this tell us about whom Jesus is?

Worship Given to Christ

NOTE: In the NWT, every time the Greek
word *"proskuneo"* is used in reference to
God, it is translated as "worship" (Rev. 5:14,
7:11, 11:16, 19:4, John 4:20, etc.), but every
time *"proskuneo"* is used in reference to
JESUS, it is translated as "obeisance"
(Matthew 14:33, 28:9, 17, Luke 24:52,
Hebrews 1:6 [see explanatory note, pp.
27–28] etc.), even though it is the same word
in the Greek [see Gr-Engl Interlinear].

Especially compare the Greek word
"proskuneo" used with reference to God in
Revelation 5:14, 7:11, 11:16, 19:4 and used
with reference to CHRIST in Matthew 14:33,
28:9, 17. Why this blatant inconsistency?

If the NWT were consistent in translating
"proskuneo" as "worship," how would these
verses referring to Christ read?

27. If Jesus is not God, why does John 5:23
require that all men should honor the Son
equally with the Father? "In order that all

may honor the Son just as they honor the Father. He that does not honor the Son does not honor the Father who sent him."

NOTE: The Greek noun τιμη (time), meaning "to honor, esteem" (Vine's Expository Dict., p. 570) is used in ascriptions of worship to God (1 Timothy 1:17; 6:16; Revelation 4:9–11; 5:13; 7:12) and to Christ (Revelation 5:12–13), and by God concerning Christ (2 Peter 1:17).

28. The Bible consistently condemns the worship of angels (e.g. Revelation 19:10). If Jesus were Michael the Archangel, why did God give instruction that all the angels should worship Him (Hebrews 1:6, cf. Revelation 5:13)? [cf. Hebrews 1:7–8: Jesus and the angels are distinct.]

29. In John 20:28, Thomas refers to Jesus in Greek as Ο κυριος μου και ο Θεος μου. This translates literally as "the Lord of me and the God of me." Why does Jesus, in John 20:29, affirm that Thomas has come to this realization? If Jesus really was not the Lord and the God of Thomas, why did Jesus not correct him for making either a false assumption or a blasphemous statement?

"Fact" to **Track**

The NWT has diluted the command to "worship" Christ in Hebrews 1:6 by

33

translating it, "Let all God's angels do obeisance to him."

However, this was not always the way in which the Watchtower Society rendered Hebrews 1:6. Back in 1970 it was all right for Jesus to receive worship. "And let all God's angels WORSHIP him" [NWT, 1970].

By 1971 it seems that Jehovah had changed His mind, or had He?

Hebrews 1:6 was changed to read: "And let all God's angels do obeisance to him" [NWT, large print, 1971]; although this footnote was added: "Or 'worship him.' Compare Hebrews 11:21."

Undeterred by their own inconsistency, the Watchtower condemned translations that render this verse as "worship" in an article in WT, 15 January 1992, p. 23. Of course they omit to own up to the fact that they translated it like that for many years.

Also, although today a Jehovah's Witness must not worship Jesus, in 1916 they were told that many would worship Charles T. Russell: "Charles Taze Russell, thou hast, by the Lord, been crowned a king... and thy enemies shall come and worship at thy feet" [ZWTR, 1 December 1916, p. 6015].

Did they really believe that Russell was *more important* than Jesus?

"Fact" to Track...

A most revealing Watchtower publication is an interlinear translation called "The Kingdom Interlinear Translation of the Greek Scriptures," published in 1969, in which the Watchtower's distortions can be clearly seen—especially their alterations to the text in which Jesus is called "God." As a damage limitation exercise, the WBTS has taken this edition out of print... find *the original* if possible.

RESURRECTION OF JESUS

JWs challenge Christians with the question, "If Jesus is God, then how was Jesus dead and God alive at the same time?" As they see it, simple logic shows that Jesus could not be God. Actually, though, the sect arrives at this wrong conclusion through a rather complex blend of erroneous teachings on the nature of death, the meaning of the resurrection and the identity of Christ (cf. p. 38).

To the JW, (1) Jesus was a human incarnation of Michael the Archangel, (2) at death He disappeared into non-existence—body, soul and spirit all gone into nothingness without a shred remaining ("God disposed of Jesus' body" [WT November 15, 1991, p. 31], and (3) Christ's resurrection consisted of the Father's creating from memory an exact duplicate of Michael the Archangel, once again in angelic rather than human form.

The Resurrection of Christ

Obviously the idea of Jesus being God would not be consistent with the scenario outlined (p. 37) by the Jehovah's Witness concerning the resurrection of Jesus. Someone who no longer exists would not be around to perform the act of bringing himself out of non-existence.

To the Bible-believing Christian, on the other hand,

(1) Jesus was the Almighty God incarnate (John 1:14; Colossians 2:9; Hebrews 10:5);
(2) it was HIS BODY that died on the cross ("He being put to death in the flesh, but being made alive in the spirit" I Peter 3:18); and
(3) His resurrection consisted of Christ raising up His own body from the grave (John 2:19–21), and leaving the empty tomb as a witness to His bodily resurrection.

The crucial question is: which scenario fits the Scriptures—the JW version of events or the Christian version?

NOTE: Jesus said of His body (John 2:19–21), "I will raise it up." Therefore, He could not have gone out of existence between His death and resurrection as the Witnesses believe. Hence the question JWs raise as a supposed obstacle to Christ's deity is pointless (i.e. How was Jesus dead and God alive at the same time?). Christ had died in the flesh but was alive in the spirit.

Christ's Resurrection Body

30. In Luke 24:36–39 and in John 20:26–27, Jesus showed His disciples the wounds in His body as proof of His resurrection. If Jesus' body had been destroyed by God after He died, how could Jesus show the disciples His body which had the wounds in His hands, feet and side and claim that He is not just a spirit, "because a spirit does not have flesh and bones just as you behold that I have" (Luke 24:39)?

31. To what was Jesus referring by the term "this temple" in John 2:19–21, if He did not mean that the body which the Jews tried to destroy would be raised from the dead... and how could a "non-existent" Christ possibly raise His own body from the grave (cf. John 10:17–18)?

Definite Pointers to a Bodily Resurrection

(1) Is it POSSIBLE that Jesus Christ was raised bodily from the dead?

Since every resurrection account recorded in the Bible features a bodily resurrection (none of the persons listed below was raised as an immaterial, invisible spirit creature), then we may logically conclude that it is at least possible that Jesus was raised bodily from the dead.

- Elijah and the widow's son (1 Kings 17:22–23);
- Elisha and the Shunammite's son (2 Kings 4:32–36);
- Elisha's bones and a dead man (2 Kings 13:20–21);
- Jesus and Jairus' daughter (Matthew 9:18–25), a widow's son (Luke 7:12–15) and Lazarus (John 11:43–44);
- The resurrection from the tombs (Matthew 27:52–53);
- Peter and Tabitha (Acts 9:40);
- Paul and Eutychus (Acts 20:9–12).

(2) Is it PROBABLE that Jesus Christ was raised bodily from the dead?
Since

(i) all the resurrections recorded in the Bible are bodily in nature and no resurrection is of an immaterial nature, and

(ii) the terminology used to describe Christ's resurrection is no different to all the other bodily resurrections, we must conclude that it is more than probable that Jesus Christ was raised bodily from the dead.

(3) Was Jesus Christ ACTUALLY raised bodily from the dead?
God's Word tells us that Christ's:

- body COULD NOT be destroyed or dissolved into gases (Acts 2:25–27);
- body WAS NOT in the tomb (Luke 24:1–8);

- power was such that He could take His life back again (John 10:17–18);
- prediction was that His body would be raised in three days (John 2:18–22).

Jesus proved that His body was raised through many infallible proofs.

  (i) He showed the wounds in His body (Luke 24:39–40);

 (ii) He ate and drank before them (Luke 24:41; Acts 10:40–41);

(iii) He explicitly denied He was a spirit (Luke 24:39; John 20:24–29);

 (iv) Over 500 people saw His resurrected body (1 Corinthians 15:6);

  (v) Our bodily resurrection will be based on the pattern of Christ's bodily resurrection (Romans 8:11; Philippians 3:21).

THEREFORE: God's Word reveals that the bodily resurrection of Jesus Christ was possible, probable and actual.

THE HOLY SPIRIT

The JWs deny the Deity of the Holy Spirit, insisting that He is merely an impersonal force acting on behalf of Jehovah.

Such teaching runs contrary to Scripture, in which the Holy Spirit is presented as being a person, having the characteristics of God (e.g. Omnipresence (Psalm 139:7–10), Omniscience (Isaiah 40:13–14), Sovereignty (1 Corinthians 12:11) and Eternality (Hebrews 9:14), and doing the work of God.

In the light of the JWs' teaching, their translation of 2 Corinthians 3:17–18 is puzzling to say the least: "Now Jehovah is the Spirit; and where the spirit of Jehovah is, there is freedom. And all of us, while we with unveiled faces reflect like mirrors the glory of Jehovah, are transformed into the same image from glory to glory, exactly as done by Jehovah [the] Spirit."

The Holy Spirit

32. If the Holy Spirit is God's *impersonal* active force,

(i) why does He directly speak and refer to Himself as "I" and "me" in Acts 13:2;

(ii) how could He be referred to as "he" and "him" in John 16:7–8 and John 16:13–14;

(iii) and how can He:
- hear - John 16:13;
- speak - Ezekiel 3:24; Matthew 10:20; Acts 8:29, 10:19, 11:12, 21:11; Hebrews 3:7, 10:15–17; Revelation 2:7, 22:17;
- forbid someone to speak -Acts 16:6;
- desire - Galatians 5:17;
- be outraged - Hebrews 10:29;
- search and know - 1 Corinthians 2:10–11;
- help - John 14:16; 16:7;
- comfort - Acts 9:31;
- quicken, or give spiritual life - John 6:63;
- intercede - Romans 8:26;
- have fellowship with us- 2 Corinthians 13:14;
- remain with Christians - John 14:16–17;
- be loved - Romans 15:30;
- be tested - Acts 5:9;
- feel hurt and be grieved - Isaiah 63:10; Ephesians 4:30;

- be lied to - Acts 5:3–4;
- be blasphemed against - Mark 3:29;
  Luke 12:10;
- teach - Nehemiah 9:20; Luke 12:12;
  John 14:26, 16:13–15;
- bear witness - John 15:26; Romans
  8:16;
- give testimony to persons - Acts
  20:23;
- give the world convincing evidence,
  or convict - John 16:8;
- decide decrees - Acts 15:28;
- reveal future events - Acts 1:16;
- inspire prophecy - Hebrews 3:7;
- appoint overseers - Acts 20:28;
- send people - Acts 13:4?

NOTE: Given the last nine abilities of the Holy Spirit in the above list—and bearing in mind the miserable record of the WBTS in these areas (cf. pp. 59–84)—would the JWs not be better served by admitting, admiring, and appealing for help from this third person of the Trinity?

33. How can the JW ignore the fact that, even in his own translation of the Bible, Acts 5:3–4 demonstrate that the Holy Spirit is God? Ananias and Sapphira were accused (v. 3) of "playing false to the Holy Spirit," while in v. 4 the same sin is defined as "played false ... to God."

34. In Matthew 28:19, Jesus tells His disciples to baptize "people of all the nations ... in the name of the Father and of the Son and of the Holy Spirit." Why would the disciples be instructed to baptize in the name of anybody or anything that was not God? Do Jehovah's Witnesses follow the command of Jesus and baptize "in the name of the Father and of the Son and of the Holy Spirit?"

JW Argument . . . Use of the Neuter Gender.

The WBTS alleges that since the Bible uses neuter pronouns to describe the Holy Spirit, He must be an "it" and not a "He."

"Nowhere do we read of Jehovah God and Jesus as being referred to by neuter pronouns, which is the case in regard to the Holy Spirit." They then proceed to quote instances where the Holy Spirit is referred to as "it" in "The Complete Bible - An American Translation", 1951 edition ... i.e. John 14:16–17, Acts 2:33. [WT, January 1953, pp. 23–24].

It is correct to say that the Greek word for spirit (*pneuma*) is a neuter form. However, it is not correct to draw the conclusion that this proves the Holy Spirit is not a person. The neuter in Greek does not imply personhood or non-personhood. For example:

- the Greek word translated "demon" (*daimonion*) is also neuter. Demons are persons, even though the Greek word is neuter.

- the Greek word for "child" (*paidion*) is neuter—and children are persons, even though the Greek word is neuter.

In Greek, the personal pronoun must match the gender of the object to which it is referring. Therefore, the Holy Spirit ("spirit" being a neuter form) is given neuter pronouns. However, scholars are correct in translating the Greek neuter pronouns as the English masculine pronoun "He" (in verses such as John 14:16–17 and 1 Corinthians 12:11) to be consistent with the rules of English.

Even if the above were not true, there are occasions when the Bible does use masculine personal pronouns for the Holy Spirit. In John 16:13 the demonstrative pronoun "that one" (*ekeinos*) is used in the masculine to refer to the Holy Spirit. This may seem to conflict with the rule given above about the pronoun agreeing in gender with the noun. However, this is a figure of speech called "*heterosis*." Heterosis is the use of one gender in the place of another to emphasize something. What Jesus is emphasizing here is that the Holy Spirit is a person.

To support its erroneous teaching about the Holy Spirit, the Watchtower twists scripture, misrepresents rules of Greek grammar and employs fallacious reasoning and deceptive tactics. The Scriptures provide immense proof of the personality of the Holy Spirit.

"Fact" to Track

While the WBTS stubbornly deny the status of personality to the Holy Spirit, they are prepared to grant it to the devil.

"Is the Devil a personification or a person? ... these accounts relate to conversations between the Devil and God, and between the Devil and Jesus Christ. Both Jehovah God and Jesus Christ are persons. Can an unintelligent "force" carry on a conversation with a person? Also, the Bible calls Satan a manslayer, a liar, a father (in spiritual sense) and a ruler... only an intelligent person could fit all those descriptions." [*Awake!*, 8 December 1973, p. 271].

When the same tests for personality are applied to the Holy Spirit (i.e. He talks to other persons and Scripture gives Him names), the Holy Spirit clearly emerges as an intelligent person.

"Proof" for Truth

The WBTS refuses to acknowledge either (1) the personality or (2) the deity of the Holy Spirit, maintaining that He is nothing more than God's impersonal active force on the earth today, comparable to "wind or radio beams." [WT, 15 January 1958, pp. 42–43].

The elements of personality ascribed to the Holy Spirit in the Bible (listed under Question 32 and further discussed on pp. 45–48) are

sufficient proof of the personality of the Holy
Spirit.

The question of the deity of the Holy Spirit
is established by the following Scriptural
truths.

(1) Scripture calls the Holy Spirit "God."
Acts 5:3–4, 2 Corinthians 3:17–18 (see
tremendous quote on p. 43).

*(2) The Bible ascribes Divine Attributes to the
Holy Spirit.*
- He is ETERNAL - Hebrews 9:14;
- He is OMNIPRESENT - Psalm 139:7,
- He is OMNISCIENT and ALL WISE-
  1 Corinthians 2:10;
- He is OMNIPOTENT - Zechariah 4:6;
  Romans 8:11, 15:19;
- He is HOLY (and according to Isaiah
  57:15 that is the definitive attribute of
  God);
- He is JUST AND RIGHTEOUS - Isaiah
  59:17–19;
- He is GOOD - Nehemiah 9:20, cf. Mark
  10:18;
- He is TRUE - John 14:17, 15:26, 16:13;
- He is SOVEREIGN - Psalm 51:12; John
  3:8.

*(3) The Bible ascribes Divine Acts to the Holy
Spirit.*
- Creation - Genesis 1:2;
- The Resurrection of Christ - Romans
  8:11; 1 Peter 3:18;
- Regeneration - John 6:63;
- Inspiration of Scripture - 2 Timothy
  3:16; cf. 2 Peter 1:10, 11, 21.

49

(4) Scripture uses the name of the Spirit along with that of the Father and the Son in such a way as to prove His proper Deity.
Matthew 28:19; 2 Corinthians 13:14.

(5) Scripture's definition of the sin of blasphemy against the Holy Ghost and its consequences demonstrates the deity of the Holy Spirit. Matthew 12:31–32.

SALVATION

Watchtower doctrine decrees that Christ alone cannot save. His atonement does not provide salvation; it is merely a ransom paid to Jehovah God by Christ in order to remove the evil effects of Adam's sin on mankind. Man may then earn his own salvation by faith and good works [*The Harp Of God*, pp. 139–141].

The JW teaching on salvation could be summarized by rewriting Ephesians 2:8–9, "For by grace you might yet be saved through faith: and that must have something to do with yourselves, it is not entirely the gift of God; it is as a result of works, that we should boast in the society."

They admit that their "gospel" is "far different" from that of Christianity [WT, 1 Oct. 1980, p. 28].

Salvation

35. Why is official Watchtower teaching that - "All who by reason of faith in Jehovah God and in Christ Jesus dedicate themselves to do God's will and then faithfully carry out their dedication will be rewarded with everlasting life ..." [*Let God Be True*, p. 298], and "Jehovah God will justify, declare righteous, on the basis of their own merit all perfected human beings who have withstood that final, decisive test of mankind. He will adopt and acknowledge them as his sons through Jesus Christ" [*Life Everlasting in Freedom of the Sons of God*, 1966, p. 400], when Ephesians 2:8–9 and Titus 3:5 are most explicit that salvation is by faith alone in Jesus Christ alone—and not of works?

36. Why does the WBTS insist that people have to "come to Jehovah's organization for salvation" [WT, 15 November 1998, p. 21] when Jesus so emphatically states in John 14:6, "I am the way and the truth and the life. No one comes to the Father except through me?"

NOTE: It is every Christian's privilege to "know" God through a personal relationship with Jesus Christ. No human organization has any authority to obstruct that relationship. JWs need not fear leaving the Watchtower organization—to abandon that counterfeit path of approach to God in favor of the real way, the Lord Jesus Christ. He invites seekers to come to Him (Matthew 11:28), assuring them: "... the one that comes to me I will by no means drive away" (John 6:37).

37. How does the Jehovah's Witness harmonize the clear statements of Acts 2:21 and Acts 4:10–12, where Jehovah **and** Jesus are presented as the name which brings salvation, other than admitting that Jehovah and Jesus are the one God? "And everyone who calls on the name of Jehovah will be saved" (Acts 2:21) "...in the name of Jesus Christ... does this man stand here.... Furthermore, there is no salvation in anyone else, for there is not another name under heaven that has been given among men by which we must get saved" (Acts 4:10–12).

38. Why do Jehovah's Witnesses persist with their belief that the sacrifice of our Lord Jesus Christ does not guarantee everlasting life and blessing to whosoever believes in Him when Hebrews 9:12; John 3:16; 1 Peter 1:18–23 amply demonstrate that it does?

The Mediator

The Bible clearly teaches that Jesus Christ is the mediator of our salvation.

- 1 Timothy 2:5: "For there is one God, and one mediator between God and men, the man Christ Jesus;"
- Hebrews 8:6: "But now Jesus has obtained a more excellent public service, so that he is also the mediator of a correspondingly

better covenant, which has been legally
established upon better promises" (also
Hebrews 9:11–15, 22–24).

However, as far as the Watchtower is concerned, the Lord Jesus Christ is not the mediator of the "great crowd." They teach that
"the mediatorship of Jesus Christ will cease"
when the last of the 144,000 enter into the
heavenly kingdom—thus robbing the "great
crowd" of Christ as their mediator [WT, 15
November 1979, pp. 26–27]. Who, therefore,
brings salvation to the majority of Jehovah's
Witnesses?

"Your attitude towards the wheat-like
anointed 'brothers' of Christ and the treatment
you accord them will be the determining fac-
tor as to whether you go into 'everlasting cutting-off' or receive 'everlasting life'."
[WT, 1 August 1981, p. 26].

"This pastoral King tells us how a person
may be considered fit to be separated to the
side of divine favor in contrast to the goat-
like people. It is by doing good to those yet
remaining on earth of the spiritual 'brothers'
of the reigning King."

[WT, 1 January 1983, p. 13].

Summary of JW Teaching on Salvation

• The vast majority of Jehovah's Witnesses
  alive today are **not** in the new covenant

mediated by Christ, therefore He **can not** be their mediator.

- However, as everyone needs a mediator, the mediator of the "great crowd" is the 144,000 who belong to the "anointed" class.

- Therefore the "great crowd" need not be so concerned about their relationship with Jesus Christ, as with their relationship to the 144,000 (JWs).

How can the WBTS be God's organization when the Son of God has been replaced by men and women of the society?

DEATH AND ETERNITY

Jehovah's Witnesses propagate the notion of "Soul Sleep," i.e. when a believer dies, he remains in an unconscious state of existence in the grave until God resurrects him. They do not accept that the soul of a person is a separate entity that has consciousness.

They also teach that:

- "Everlasting punishment" means annihilation; therefore, the wicked will NOT be punished forever, and there is no eternal soul;
- The word "hell" (Hebrew - *Sheol*; Greek - *Hades*) means nothing more than "the grave" [*Let God Be True*, pp. 72–73];
- The teaching of an eternal hell is a "God-dishonoring doctrine" which was invented by Satan and propagated by the Babylonians, and other heathen empires [*Let God Be True*, p. 79].

Death and Eternity

39. If the spirit of a man has no existence apart from the body, why does Stephen, just before his death in Acts 7:59, pray to Jesus to "receive my spirit"? How could Jesus receive Stephen's spirit if a man's spirit ceases to exist when the body dies?

40. If the soul dies when the body dies, how could the "souls" of those who had been "slaughtered" (Revelation 6:9–11), cry out "with a loud voice, saying: 'Until when Sovereign Lord...'?" [Revelation 20:4].

41. If the human soul is the person, how could the soul go out of a person (Genesis 35:18) or come back into a person (1 Kings 17:21–22)?

42. If the soul is no more than the life of the person, why does:

(i) Uriah show that the soul is more than life when he states: "As you are living and as your soul is living" (2 Samuel 11:11);

(ii) 3 John 2 make a clear distinction between the good health of the life and the welfare of the soul?

43. Jesus uses the phrase "Truly I say to you, ..." over fifty times in the Bible. In the NWT, the comma is placed after the word "you" every time **except** in Luke 23:43, where the comma is placed after the word "today." "And he said to him: 'Truly I tell you today, You will be with me in Paradise'." Why is the comma placed after "today" instead of after "you" in this verse? If the translation of this phrase in Luke 23:43 were consistent with how it is translated in all the other verses in which it appears, and the comma was placed after the word "you," how would it read?

44. If, when a believer dies, he remains in an unconscious state of existence in the grave until God resurrects him, how can:

  (i) Abraham, Isaac, and Jacob "all [be] living to him (God)" (Luke 20:37–38), since they had died hundreds of years before Jesus said this?

 (ii) the dead be "happy" and find "rest" (Revelation 14:13)?

(iii) 1 Thess. 5:10 state, "He died for us, that, whether we stay awake or are asleep, we should live together with him"?.

NOTE: These Scriptures demonstrate that in death and life we have direct communication with God (also 2 Corinthians 5:1–10; Philippians 1:20–24).

45. In John 8:56, Jesus says, "Abraham your father rejoiced greatly in the prospect of seeing my day, and he saw it and rejoiced." Since Abraham died hundreds of years before Jesus said this, how could Jesus say that

Abraham "saw it and rejoiced," if there is no conscious awareness after death?

46. On the Hebrew word *Sheol.*

(i) Referring to Isaiah 14:9–17, if there is no conscious awareness after death
  • how could *Sheol* "... become agitated at you in order to meet you on coming in..." (v. 9);
  • how could the souls in *Sheol* "...speak up and say to you..." (vv. 10–11);
  • how could the souls in *Sheol* when "...seeing you will gaze even at you; they will give close examination even to you, [saying,] 'Is this the man" (vv. 16–17) - and how would you be aware that this was happening?

(ii) What are "the distressing circumstances of *Sheol*" spoken of in Psalm 116:3, if *Sheol* is an area of unconsciousness?

47. On the Greek word *Hades.*

If *Hades* were simply the place of the unconscious, why is the rich man in *Hades* depicted as lifting his eyes, existing in torments, being able to see Abraham, and crying out (Luke 16:23–24)? [Surely **not** the kind of activity you would associate with anyone with no conscious existence.]

48. What is the meaning of Revelation 14:9–11, which warns, "... If anyone worships the wild beast ... he shall be tormented with fire and sulfur ... And the smoke of their torment ascends forever and ever...." How could "anyone" be "tormented... forever and ever" if annihilation is the order of the day?

Everlasting punishment

49. Why is the NWT content to translate the Greek verb κολαζο "punish" when it is used in Acts 4:21, but insists on rendering its derivative term – κολαδις - as "cutting-off" in Matthew 25:46?

"And these will depart into everlasting cutting-off, but the righteous ones into everlasting life."

"Fact" to Track

You cannot claim everlasting life and deny everlasting punishment.

According to the JW way of thinking, Jesus orders the "goats" a way into "everlasting cutting-off"... therefore they will not endure eternal torment, but will instead be immediately annihilated.

The Greek language does not permit that interpretation of the text. The term "everlasting" [Gr, αιωυιος (*aionios*)] is used to describe the duration of both the future state of the righteous and of the wicked. If "everlasting life" is life without end; life that will never cease, then "everlasting cutting-off" [or, more properly, "punishment"] must be punishment without end—punishment that will never cease.

"Quote" to Note

When κολαδις appears again in I John 4:18, the NWT translates it "restraint"—a term of correction, not annihilation.

50. The Bible records that two individuals (the beast and the false prophet) will be cast alive into a lake of fire burning with brimstone (Revelation 19:20). After this event, Christ will reign on earth for 1000 years (Revelation 20:1–6), and when Satan and his forces are defeated at the end of that 1000 years, the Devil will be "hurled into the lake of fire and sulfur, where both the wild beast and the false prophet [already there]; and they will be tormented day and night forever and ever" (Revelation 20:10). Why is it that, although 1000 years have passed, the beast and the false prophet are still in the lake of fire and brimstone? No annihilation has taken place.

An examination of the Watchtower teaching on death and eternity reveals the fact that once again, the JWs have attempted to distort the normal sense of Scripture in an effort to prop up their own faulty theology.

The Scriptures do NOT support:

(1) the notion that man does not have an immortal soul, but would merely be a

memory in the mind of God, waiting to be remembered and restored;

(2) the definitions given to *Hades* or *Sheol* by the WBTS (i.e. "the common grave of dead mankind" [*Reasoning*, p. 169];

(3) the belief that "everlasting punishment" equals a cutting-off or annihilation.

While it may be comfortable to have a gospel without hell and thus substitute the choice of annihilation or eternal life in the place of everlasting punishment or eternal life, this is **not** the alternative that is presented in the gospel of Christ. The biblical position is that if we live without repentance of our sin and refuse to accept the forgiveness and love of God as manifested in Christ, we condemn ourselves to an eternal hell.

That truth should be a sufficient spur to compel us to share the gospel with the self-styled Jehovah's Witness who appears at our door.

THE END TIMES

The JWs have a quite unique eschatology.

- Jesus Christ returned as an invisible spirit being in the autumn of 1914 [WT, 15 June 1979, p. 23].
- Dead JWs were raised from their sleep in the graves to join Him in the spiritual temple [*Let God Be True*, p. 203].
- A three-and-a-half year struggle followed until 1918, when the two witnesses were slain.
- From 1919 on, the Holy Spirit—to them an impersonal force—was poured out in fulfillment of Joel 2:28–32.
- This age will soon end with the battle of Armageddon in which all who are not JWs will be slaughtered.
- The 144,000 will then reign in heaven; the "other sheep" will be on earth for the millennial age [*Let God Be True*, pp. 256–257].

The End Times
The 144,000

51. The Watchtower Society teaches that the 144,000 of Revelation 7:4 is to be taken literally. If ALL of Revelation 7 is to be taken literally, then from where does the Bible say that the 144,000 will come? (Rev. 7:5–8)

52. Watchtower doctrine insists that only 144,000 are "born of God."

(i) Why does 1 John 5:1 insist that **all** Christians are "born of God": "everyone believing that Jesus is the Christ has been born from God."?

(ii) Hebrews 3:1 refers to "holy brothers, partakers of the heavenly calling." In Mark 3:35, Jesus says, "Whoever does the will of God, this one is my brother." Therefore, according to the Bible, whoever does the will of God is a brother of Jesus and a partaker of the heavenly calling. How can this be if the Watchtower Society teaches that only 144,000 people go to heaven?

53. Hebrews 11:16, in speaking about some of the faithful people of the Old Testament (Abel, Noah, Abraham, etc.) says, "But now they are reaching out for a better [place], that is, one belonging to heaven..." and "... their God for he has made a city ready for them." The footnote on the word "city" refers to the heavenly Jerusalem of Hebrews 12:22 and Revelation 21:2. How can this be since according to the teachings of the Watchtower Society, the only people who will go to heaven are the 144,000 spirit-anointed who have been chosen from people who either lived after Christ died [*Paradise*, p. 231] or have been gathered in since 1931 [*Paradise*, p. 195]?

54. If there are 144,000 spirit anointed people who have a heavenly hope, and a great crowd of people who have another hope of everlasting life on paradise Earth,

(i) Why does Paul say that there is only **One** hope (Ephesians 4:4), instead of two?

(ii) Why does Jesus say that the "other sheep" would be brought into the "one flock with one shepherd" (John 10:16)? (Obviously that flock assemble in the one location. Ephesians 2:11–16 explains that the "other sheep" are converted Gentiles who would become "one body" with converted Jews, through the person and work of the Lord Jesus Christ. There is no place for two distinct groups to exist apart from one another).

Position of the Great Crowd
55. According to Watchtower teaching, the "great crowd/other sheep" do not have a heavenly future, but an earthly one. However:

(i) Where does Revelation 19:1 position this great crowd?

(ii) Revelation 7:9, 15 positions the great

crowd "before the throne." Since "before the throne" is where "all the angels were standing" to worship God (Revelation 7:11) and "before the throne" is the place from which "a new song" sounded "out of heaven" (Revelation 14:2–3), where does that mean the great crowd will be?

(iii) Revelation 7:15 uses another phrase which further helps us to locate the "great crowd": they are rendering service to God day and night "in his temple" (i.e. God's habitation). Therefore, where is this great crowd?

"Fact" to Track

All the Biblical evidence demonstrates that the 144,000 **cannot** be who the WBTS say they are.

JWs argue that:

(1) Luke 12:32 shows only a "little flock" shall inherit the kingdom.

(2) Revelation 7:1–8 and 14:1–5 show this "little flock" to number 144,000 and Revelation 5:9–10 further reveals that they will rule as "kings and priests." In their publication, *Make Sure Of All Things*, (1965, p. 303), the WBTS speaks of "144,000 redeemed from Earth to be Kings and Priests with Christ in Heaven" (Rev. 14:1, 4; Rev. 5:9–10).

(3) The 144,000 are in direct contrast to the "great crowd" who do not have a heavenly future but an earthly one. John

10:16 and Revelation 7:9–17 show that
this earthly group is called "other sheep"
or "great crowd."

(4) During the millennium, when the earth is
a paradise, all those counted worthy of a
resurrection (John 5:28–29) will have an
opportunity to learn obedience and loyalty to the organizational structures that
God establishes through the 144,000 and
Jesus Christ reigning in heaven
(Revelation 20:11–15).

In actual fact, Scripture says the very opposite to this. For example, the Bible does **not**
identify the people mentioned in Revelation
7:1–8 and 5:9–10 as being the same people at
all; they are decidedly different.

- Revelation 7:4 identifies the 144,000 as
coming "from every tribe of the sons of
Israel,"
- while the priests and kings of Revelation
5:9, who will rule over the earth, come
"out of every tribe and tongue and people and nation."

Therefore those in Revelation 5:9–10 are
not the 144,000. A comparison with the
words of Revelation 7:9 will reveal that they
are actually the great crowd. It is the great
crowd who comes "out of all nations and
tribes and peoples and tongues."

"Date" to State ...

It is interesting to muse over how the Watchtower Society is able to work out how many places of the 144,000 were still vacant when the required number began to be filled up in Charles Russell's day. Evidently they had considerable difficulty with this.

- In a book published in 1958 we are told that the number was complete in 1931 [*Paradise*, p. 195];
- A different Watchtower publication [*Man's Salvation Out Of World Distress At Hand*, 1975, p. 302] identifies 1935 as the year when the number was completed.

Faced with such contradictory information, it is surely extremely difficult for any JW to trust the Watchtower on this one.

The Return of Christ

56. How can Jesus return invisibly, or spiritually, to earth when He never went away invisibly (cf. John 14:3 with Matthew 28:20)?

NOTE: This is precisely what Charles Russell argued in ZWTR in 1879. It is obvious that originally Russell and his followers were expecting a physical return—not a spiritual, invisible return of Jesus.

The Watchtower Society has performed another of its customary "U-turns" on this doctrine of Christ's Second Coming.

- In relation to this subject, the

Watchtower taught in 1879 that the verse, " 'If I go away, I will come again,' *cannot* refer to a spiritual coming *again*, because, spiritually, He never went away, as He said, 'Lo, I am with you always, even to the end of the world' [age]. Therefore, Jesus taught his *second* PERSONAL *coming*."
[ZWTR, July 1879, p. 4].

- However, JW doctrine had changed direction entirely by 1979. "According to the 'sign' that Jesus foretold and also according to certain Bible time measurements, his invisible 'presence,' or *parousia*, began in autumn of 1914 CE."
[WT, 15 June 1979, p. 23]

57. If Christ will not have a visible return to earth,

(i) how will He be seen by "ALL the tribes of the earth" (Matthew 24:30) and by "**every** eye" (Revelation 1:7) when He returns?

(ii) Hebrews 9:28, speaking of Christ, says, "... and the second time he appears...." How can Christ appear a second time if He will not have a visible return to earth?

(iii) how will He fulfill the promise of the angels in Acts 1:9–11: "And after he had said these things, while they were looking on, he was lifted up and a cloud caught him up from their vision. And as they were gazing into the sky while he was on his way, also, look. two men in white garments stood alongside them, and they said: 'Men of Galilee, why do you stand looking into the sky? This Jesus who was received up from you into the sky will come thus in the same manner as you have beheld him going into the sky'?"

NOTE: "In the same manner" must mean that Jesus began with His feet on the ground then went up in the air into the clouds, and therefore will return from the clouds, through the air until His feet once again are touching the ground.

58. How can JWs insist that the *parousia* took place in 1914, when Jehovah informs us in 1 Thessalonians 4:15–17 that both dead and living saints will be caught away together to meet the Lord in the air?

"For this is what we tell you by Jehovah's word, that we the living who survive to the presence [παρονδια (*parousia*)] of the Lord shall in no way precede those who have fallen asleep [in death]; because the Lord himself will descend from heaven with a commanding call, with an archangel's voice and with God's trumpet, and those who are dead in union with Christ will rise first. Afterward we the living who are surviving will, together [footnote: at the same time] with them, be caught away in clouds to meet the Lord in the air; and thus we shall always be with [the] Lord."

"Fact" to Track

The Greek word παρονδια *(parousia,* "coming") is used twenty-four times in the New Testament:

- seventeen times of Christ,
- once of the lawless one,
- and six times about other people.

Since all six occurrences of the word *parousia* when used in connection with other people speak of a bodily presence (1 Corinthians 16:17; 2 Corinthians 7:6, 7:7, 10:10; Philippians 1:26, 2:12), why should the same not be true of Christ's *parousia*?

NOTE: these References Concerning Christ and Parousia

- 2 Peter 1:16... bodily presence of the Lord on the earth, up to A.D. 33.
- 1 Thessalonians 4:15–16... descended from heaven NOT enthroned in heaven
- Matthew 24:27... lightning in the sky (everyone will know).
- Matthew 24:37–39... a sweeping away (all alive will know).
- Matthew 24:40–41... one taken and the other left: no instances of that being reported in 1914.
- 2 Thessalonians 2:8... the lawless one done away with and brought to nothing.
- James 5:7... no need of patience after the *parousia*: full fruit arrived.

59. If Jesus Christ is Michael the Archangel, how can Matthew write of the "son of man arriving in his glory, and all the

. angels with him"? (25:31). Since "all the angels" would certainly include Michael the Archangel, is it possible that Jesus could return *with himself*?

When Will it Happen?

60. Since Acts 1:7 and other scriptures (Matthew 24:36, 25:13; Mark 13:32; 1 Thessalonians 5:1–2) emphasize the fact that we cannot predict the date for the second coming of Christ or the end of the world, why is the history of the Watchtower Society pockmarked with failed predictions for these events?

"Fact" to Track

Pages 79–114, under the headings, "False Prophecies" and "Doctrinal Somersaults," list many dates that became the subject of Watchtower predictions and yet turned out to be miserable hoaxes.

That any organization could make such claims is incredible—especially one claiming to be God's "faithful and discreet servant."

One of the key dates in JW chronology is 607 B.C. ...

"Date" to State ...
The Crucial Date of 607 B.C. Exposed.

In Watchtower chronology the importance of the year 1914 cannot be overstated.

According to the organization's prophecies, all governments were to have been overthrown and dissolved, and Christ Jesus was to have actively taken up his Kingdom power and begun to rule invisibly to human eyes by October 1914.

This 1914 date was selected as the result of an exceptionally complex, and bizarre, series of calculations.

The 2,520 Mystery Number
The Watchtower decided that "the times of the Gentiles" referred to by Christ in Luke 21:24:

(i) BEGAN when Jerusalem was destroyed by the Babylonians under Nebuchadnezzar (WBTS maintain that occurred in 607 B.C.)

(ii) and ENDED some 2,520 years later, i.e. 1914.

[The figure of 2,520 years was obtained by assuming that the "seven times" of Daniel 4:25 were actually 2,520 *days* (cf. Revelation 12:6, 14), which they then managed to transform into 2,520 calendar *years*].

There are IMMENSE PROBLEMS with that dating system.

Leaving aside the quite ridiculous "exegesis" of Scripture employed by the JWs, the 607 B.C. date is disputed by all archaeological evidence.

Mr. Raymond Franz, (a former member of the WBTS "Governing Body" and nephew of a past President of the Watchtower, Frederick Franz), testified to his inability to find any evidence to support the date 607 B.C. during an extensive study he conducted while a member of the WBTS.

"Months of research were spent on this one subject of 'Chronology' and it resulted in the longest article in the *Aid* publication. Much of the time was spent endeavoring to find some proof, some backing in history, for the 607 B.C.E. date so crucial to our calculations for 1914.

"Charles Ploeger, a member of the headquarters staff, was at the time serving as a secretary for me and he searched through the libraries of the New York City area for anything that might substantiate that date historically. We found absolutely nothing in support of 607 B.C.E."

[Ray Franz, *Crisis Of Conscience*, p. 25].

On page 140 of Mr. Franz's book, this statement appears:

"The research I had to do in connection with the book *Aid To Bible Understanding* brought home to me that the Society's date of 607 B.C.E. for Jerusalem's destruction by Babylon was contradicted by all known historical evidence. Still, I continued to put trust in that date in spite of the evidence, feeling that it had scriptural backing. Without 607

B.C.E. the crucial date of 1914 would be placed in question. I took the view that the historical evidence was likely defective...."

Disfellowshipped for Telling the Truth

In 1977, Carl Olof Jonsson, an elder from Sweden, with twenty-five years of loyal service to the Jehovah's Witnesses, sent a colossal amount of research he had done in Bible-related chronology to the Watchtower Headquarters in Bethel, Brooklyn, NY.

Jonsson tried to alert the Governing Body to the weakness in the Society's chronological calculations leading to the 1914 date. He had substantiated that Jerusalem fell in 587–586 B.C. and NOT in 607 B.C.. For his efforts, Mr. Jonsson was privately classified as "demon-possessed" and publicly condemned. He was eventually "disfellowshipped" in July 1982.

Not the Slightest Support for the Date

Writing later in *The Gentile Times Reconsidered*, Jonsson noted:

"Evidently the Watch Tower Society realizes that all the evidence discovered hitherto since the middle of the last century unanimously points to 587 B.C.E. instead of 607 B.C.E. as the eighteenth year of Nebuchadnezzar. Among the thousands of discovered documents from the Neo-Babylonian era, they have not been able to find the slightest support for their 607 B.C.E. date; hence, the reference to 'yet undiscovered material'.

"A chronology that has to be based on 'yet undiscovered material,' because it is demolished by the discovered material, is resting on a weak foundation indeed."

FALSE PROPHECIES

It is rather ironic that the Watchtower Society itself has condemned "false prophesying."

An article in *Awake!* states: "true, there have been those in times past who predicted an 'end to the world,' even announcing a specific date. The "end" did not come. They were guilty of false prophesying. Why? What was missing? Missing was the full measure of evidence required in fulfillment of Bible prophecy. Missing from such people were God's truths and the evidence that he was guiding and using them" [*Awake!* 8 Ocotber 1968, p. 23].

Truth is, the Watchtower has the dubious distinction of not having any of their numerous prophecies fulfilled in over 100 years.

The Watchtower Society stands self-condemned.

Examples of false prophecies that have been made by the Watchtower are plentiful: I have documented evidence of failed predictions from the Watchtower that runs to 120 pages.

Some of the more "classic" ones include:

(1) The Pyramid Theory.

Charles Taze Russell devoted the 10th study in his book, *Thy Kingdom Come*, to the Great Pyramid of Egypt. He had been searching for new prophecy to set before his followers. This is what he settled upon.

Study X
The Testimony of God's Stone Witness and Prophet, The Great Pyramid in Egypt

General description of the Great Pyramid; Why of special interest to Christians; The Great Pyramid a storehouse of truth, scientific, historic and prophetic; Bible allusions to it...

Russell used the measurements of the Great Pyramid of Giza to arrive at various prophetic dates. One example of Russell's measurement (and consequent prophecy) from that pyramid is detailed in *Thy Kingdom Come*, 1891, pp. 342, 362:

"Then measuring down the 'Entrance Passage' from that point, to find the distance to the entrance of the 'Pit,' representing the great trouble and destruction with which this age is to close, when evil will be overthrown from power, we find it to be 3,416 inches, symbolizing 3,416 years from the above date, B.C. 1542. This calculation shows A.D. 1874 as marking the beginning of the period of trouble; for 1542 years B.C. plus 1874 years A.D. equals 3,416 years.

"Thus the Pyramid witnesses that the close of 1874 was the chronological beginning of the time of trouble such as was not since there was a nation no, nor ever shall be afterwards. And thus it will be noted that this 'Witness' fully corroborates the Bible testimony on this subject.

"Its wonderful correspondences with the Bible leave no room for doubt that the same divine inspirer of the prophets and apostles inspired this 'Witness' also."

Therefore the founder of the WBTS (and its first President), who is supposed to have been used exclusively by God as His prophet in modern times, used "pyramidology" to provide dates for his prophetic speculations.

NOTE: Russell's measurement (detailed on page 80) was the length of an interior passageway discovered inside the Pyramids. It has absolutely NO substantiation in Scripture.

Prophecy Fails.
It should come as no surprise to discover that the particular measurements of the Pyramid that pointed to the year 1874 as the beginning of the time of trouble proved to be a failure.

In order to save face, Russell simply changed the measurements in later editions of his book and therefore extended the time period. The original "*3,416* inches" mysteriously becomes "*3,457* inches," thus advancing the date from A.D. 1874 to A.D. 1914.

Yet Zion's Watch Tower had stated: "We see no reason for changing the figures nor could we change them if we would. They are, we believe, God's dates, not ours. But bear in mind that the end of 1914 is not the date for the beginning, but for the end of the time of trouble." [ZWTR, 15 July 1894, p. 226]

Nor was Russell finished with the Pyramid. He later determined, by the length of the corridors in the Pyramid, that the saints would be raptured in 1910. [*Studies in the Scriptures* Vol. III; *Thy Kingdom Come*, 1891, p. 364, in versions issued before 1910]. That did NOT happen either.

A Cover-Up.

However, modern Watchtower material attempts to hide this debacle from their followers by misquoting their own literature to present Russell and his early study group in a favorable light. [cf. WT, 1 July 1973, p. 402].

Another false prophecy from the Watchtower concerns:

(2) *The obliteration of Christianity in 1918*

The WBTS taught: "In the year 1918... Christendom shall go down as a system to oblivion..." [*The Finished Mystery*, 1917, p. 513].

NOTE: In the last volume of *Studies in the Scriptures* the date for the end of the world was further advanced to 1918. The Watchtower Society arrived at that date using the following fanciful method:

Seven prophetic times of 360 years each made 2,520 years. This beginning with the removal of King Zedekiah in 605 B.C. produces the year 1914. It was later suggested that as Ezekiel was dumb for one year, five months and twenty-six days, so the end would come after Charles Taze Russell's dumbness in death, i.e. on April 27, 1918.

Needless to say, like all the other dates the Watchtower organization has foisted upon its adherents, the prophesied event did not take place, the end of the world did not come, and Christianity was not obliterated.

(3) *Old Testament men returning to Earth*

According to Watchtower predictions, the year 1925 was meant to be the time when Old Testament saints, [like Abraham, Isaac, Jacob,

David, the heroes of faith (Hebrews 11), etc.], would return to earth.

- "We may expect 1925 to witness the return of these faithful men of Israel from the condition of death, being resurrected. 1925 will mark the return of Abraham, Isaac, Jacob, and the faithful prophets of old."
  [*Millions Now Living Will Never Die*, 1920, pp. 88–90].

So Definite a Date.

No uncertainty was expressed anywhere concerning this prediction made by the Watchtower Bible and Tract Society over several years.

- "There will be no slip-up ... Abraham should enter upon the actual possession of his promised inheritance in the year 1925 A.D." [WT, 15 October 1917, p. 157].
- "1925 is definitely settled by the Scriptures." [WT, 1 April 1923, p. 106].
- "The year 1925 is a date definitely and clearly marked in the Scriptures, even more clearly than that of 1914." [WT, 15 July 1924, p. 211].

In fact, the Watchtower clearly stated in 1922 their claimed source of this chronological information: "This chronology is not of man, but of God." [WT, 15 July 1922, p. 217]

and yet Abraham, Isaac and Jacob did not return bodily in 1925. It was *another* false prophecy.

Beth-Sarim Constructed

Even though the anticipated return had not taken place by 1929, it was still a topic of much excited anticipation among JWs.

For this reason, Rutherford, realizing that when Abraham and company finally did show up they would need accommodation, gave instructions to build them a house. In his book, *Salvation,* Rutherford mentions this house and the reason behind its construction.

"At San Diego, California, there is a small piece of land, on which, in the year 1929, there was built a house, which is called and known as Beth-Sarim. The Hebrew words *Beth-Sarim* mean 'House of the Princes'; and the purpose of acquiring that property and building the house was that there might be some tangible proof that there are those on earth today who fully believe God and Christ Jesus and in His kingdom, and who believe that the faithful men of old will soon be resurrected by the Lord, be back on earth, and take charge of the visible affairs of earth." [*Salvation,* 1939, p. 311]

In his last book, Rutherford again mentioned Beth-Sarim, confirming the reason for its construction and the continued expectation of JWs of its occupancy by the Old Testament saints: "In this expectation the house at

San Diego, California, which house has been much publicized with malicious intent by the religious enemy, was built, in 1930, and named 'Beth-Sarim,' meaning 'House of the Princes.' It is now held in trust for the occupancy of those princes on their return." [*The New World*, p. 104]

Get Out While the Going's Good.

It should be pointed out that Judge Rutherford spent the last years of his life in this beautiful mansion while his followers suffered poverty during the Great Depression of the 1930's, and even though the original deed of the property (dated 24 December 1929) required that "this property and premises being dedicated to Jehovah and the use of his kingdom it shall be used as such for ever," Beth-Sarim was disposed of in 1948 and the teaching concerning the "return of the ancient worthies was quietly dropped in 1950." [*Millions Now Living Will Never Die: A Study of Jehovah's Witnesses*, Alan Rogerson, p. 48]

Therefore, Beth-Sarim's stint in kingdom service was more than a few years short of perpetual.

ARTICLE IN TIME MAGAZINE

"Judge Joseph Frederick Rutherford, 60, lives in a ten room Spanish mansion, No 4440 Braeburn Rd, San Diego, CA. Last week he deeded No 4440 Braeburn Road, and adjacent two car garage and a pair of automobiles to King David, Gideon, Barak, Samson,

Jephthae, Samuel and sundry other mighty men of ancient Palestine. Positive is he that they are shortly to reappear on earth, said he: 'I have purposely landscaped the place with palm and olive trees so that these princes of the universe will feel at home'."

[*Time Magazine*, March 31,1930].

There is a Very Revealing Epilogue to This Story.
In 1975 the Watchtower Society published a book which mentioned Beth-Sarim. However, the information contained in its pages only serves to complicate the Jehovah's Witnesses historical credibility. From its very inception, Beth-Sarim was said to have been built for Abraham and friends; this book appears to tell a completely different story.

"In time, a direct contribution was made for the purpose of constructing a house in San Diego for Brother Rutherford's use. It was not built at the expense of the Watchtower Society. Concerning this property, the 1939 book *Salvation* stated: 'At San Diego, California, there is a small piece of land, on which, in the year 1929, there was built a house, which is called and known as Beth-Sarin'." [*1975 Yearbook of Jehovah's Witnesses*, p. 194]

There are Two Problems With this Yearbook Statement.

   (1) First, the Watchtower claimed that it was built for Brother Rutherford's use when in fact, according to Rutherford himself, it was built for the Old Testament saints.

   (2) Second, the writer of the Yearbook articles quotes (or, more accurately, misquotes) Rutherford, making Rutherford say the very opposite to what he did say.

The author of the *Yearbook* quotes the *Salvation* book, written by Rutherford, which mentions Beth-Sarim. However, he only gives a partial quotation, and, conveniently, stops just short of the truth. I have given the full quote from the *Salvation* book on page 85. In comparing the two quotes (*Salvation*, 1939, p. 311 and *1975 Yearbook of Jehovah's Witnesses*, p. 194), it will be extremely obvious how the Watchtower has lied.

Compounding the problems of failed predictions, the Watchtower Society has, in its attempts to cover-up embarrassing events in their past, turned from false prophecies to blatant lying. Perhaps worst of all is the fact that in so doing, they are now lying to their own loyal followers.

"Fact" to Track

At the end of the Watchtower Society's latest "History" book (*Jehovah's Witnesses, Proclaimers of God's Kingdom* 1993), there is a chronological section called "Notable Dates." The prediction for 1925 does not even get a mention.

(4) World wars and space rockets.

The Watchtower could not even get historical predictions correct.

(i) After France was lost to Germany in 1940, the Watchtower president Joseph F. Rutherford stated that Britain would also fall to the Nazis. [*Judge Rutherford Uncovers Fifth Column*, July 1940, p. 15]

(ii) "Man cannot by airplane or rockets or other means get above the air envelope which is about our earthly globe...." [*The Truth Shall Make You Free*, p. 285, 1943 edition]

Admittedly, many people (including some prominent scientists) also claimed that men could never leave the earth's atmosphere by rockets, but we are not dealing with science here. It has been made clear, not only by Watchtower publications, but by the Watchtower's own leaders, that their information comes directly from God therefore it has to be correct. A scientist can be excused for getting it wrong; God cannot.

The Acid Test of Prophecy

If God had given any of these "prophetic words," they should easily pass the test of a true prophet outlined in Deuteronomy 18:21–22:

"And if thou say in thine heart, How shall we know the word which the LORD hath not spoken? When a prophet speaketh in the name of the LORD, if the thing follow not, nor come to pass, that [is] the thing which the LORD hath not spoken, [but] the prophet hath spoken it presumptuously: thou shalt not be afraid of him."

To be a prophet of God, each and every single one of the prophecies made must come completely true, or else the prophet making it (in this case, the Watchtower Bible and Tract Society) is a false prophet and therefore is not of God.

Even the WT will admit that. I read, with great interest, the Watchtower article of 15 May 1930, p. 154, which expressed the opinion that a true prophet's words will come to pass exactly as prophesied. If it does not come to pass, the prophet is a false prophet.

"It matters not whether he proclaims his message with deliberate, willful and malicious intent to deceive, or whether he is the blinded and deluded dupe of Satan and hence unwittingly used of him. In either case, he is a false prophet and hence the agent of Satan."

More False Prophecies.

Fine though those words are, failure in the realm of prophecy did not cause the Watchtower Society to confess their deluded and duped state, or to cease from the practice of making further predictions. Their mistakes did not even have the basic effect of teaching them to exercise extreme caution in this area.

Countless pages of failed prophecies have been collated by various parties to emphasize how consistently wrong the Watchtower "prophecies" have been throughout its history. This organization, which more than 5 million Jehovah's Witnesses believe to be "God's channel" of communication to mankind, is strangely also the organization with a monu-mental record of failed predictions. It has consistently missed the target for over 120 years.

In this context, words printed in the 1 April edition of the Watchtower, 1972, are most illuminating:

"Of course, it is easy to say that this group acts as a 'prophet' of God. It is another thing to prove it. The only way that this can be done is to review the record. What does it show?" [WT, 1 April 1972, p. 197]

That question has received a most resound-ing answer.

God's Verdict

God is definite in His righteous judgment against false prophets: He declares His oppo-sition to prophets who make false predictions in His name (Deuteronomy 18:21–22; Jeremiah 28; Ezekiel 13:8).

The Watchtower has made false prophecies on countless occasions, therefore the conclusion must be drawn that God, by His own decree, is against the Watchtower and thereby condemns this organization. Jehovah cannot take any pleasure in these self-styled "Witnesses."

DOCTRINAL SOMERSAULTS

Jehovah's Witnesses remind us of those who the Bible describes as, "... children, tossed to and fro, and carried about with every wind of doctrine" (Ephesians 4:14).

There are so many blatant, glaring inconsistencies in Watchtower teaching. To read through their official literature is to encounter doctrinal somersault after doctrinal somersault.

Of course, if it were true that Jehovah God is the editor of the *Watchtower* and the *Watchtower* is His word without any qualification whatsoever (as Presidents Franz and Knorr respectively swore under oath), then there would not be any inconsistencies and certainly no need to change anything that has ever been published by the Watchtower.

Consider some of the many inconsistencies that have surfaced at different junctures in the relatively brief history of the JWs.

(1) Statement of when 6,000 years of human history would be complete.

- 6,000 years of human history ended in 1873. [*Studies in the Scriptures*, 1889 Vol. 2, p. 39]
- 6,000 years of human history ended in 1972. [*The Truth Shall Make You Free*, p. 152, 1943 edition]
- 6,000 years of human history ended in 1975. [WT, 1 May 1967, p. 262; *Awake!*, 8 October 1968]

(2) Date for Armageddon.

- Armageddon would end in 1914. [*The Time is At Hand*, p. 101, 1889 Edition]
- Armageddon would end in 1915. [*The Time is At Hand*, p. 101, 1915 Edition]
- Armageddon is "just ahead" (1933). [J.F. Rutherford, *Salvation*, 1939, pp. 310–361]
- Armageddon is "just ahead" (1940). [*The Messenger*, September 1940, p. 6]
- "The war of Armageddon is nearing its breaking-out point" (1955). [*You May Survive Armageddon Into God's New World*, 1955, p. 331]

Today, Jehovah's Witnesses expect Armageddon at any minute. Given the crazy sequence of failed predictions indicated above, is it a surprise to discover that the JWs

have "opened out" their date for
Armageddon?

(3) When the millennium began.
- The Millennium began in 1873. [*Thy
  Kingdom Come*, p. 305]
- The Millennium began in 1874.
  [*Finished Mystery*, p. 386]

(4) The book of Ruth..
- The Book of Ruth is "not prophetical."
  [*Watchtower Reprints IV*, p. 3110,
  Nov.15, 1902].
- The Book of Ruth "is prophetic."
  [Watchtower Book, *Preservation*, pp.
  169, 175–176]

(5) Will the men of Sodom and Gomorrah receive a second opportunity?
Among the questions that have raged in
Jehovah's Witness circles for over a century is
this one: Will the men of Sodom be resurrected? Witness the official - and changing -
answer(s) of the Watchtower to that question:

- YES, according to *The Watchtower*, July
  1879, p. 8.
- NO, according to *The Watchtower*, June
  1, 1952, p. 338.
- YES, according to *The Watchtower*,
  August 1, 1965, p. 479.
- NO, according to *The Watchtower*, June
  1,1988, p. 31.
- YES, according to the Watchtower

Society's *Live Forever* book (old edition, 1982) p. 179.

- NO, according to the Watchtower Society's *Live Forever* book (new edition, 1989) p. 179.
- YES, according to the Watchtower Society's *Insight* book, Vol.2, p. 985.
- NO, according to the Watchtower Society's *Revelation Climax* book, p. 273.

JWs will wriggle out of that with the excuse, "We used to believe in that, but we got some further revelation and we do not believe that any more. The light gets brighter as the years go by." *

"The light gets brighter" is a misquotation of Proverbs 4:18: "But the path of the just [is]as the shining light, that shineth more and more unto the perfect day."

New Truth Does Not Contradict Old Truth.
The JW is trying to say that God slowly reveals His truth to His people, and truth becomes clearer as we reach the end of "the system." That is actually a half-truth, for while knowledge from God may increase (i.e. from Old to New Testament times), it certainly will not contradict what has been already revealed.

"The light gets brighter and brighter as time goes on," says the JW. The difficulty (as more than one has pointed out) is that the light is blinking on and off with such regularity that

---

*That is no less than eight "oscillations" within 100 years.

reading Watchtower material is like sitting in front of flashing traffic signals.

"Quote" to **Note**

The tendency of the Watchtower Society not only to misquote the writings of others, but to modify their own publications, is illustrated in the following quotations from different editions of the same book, *Live Forever*, pp. 178–180, paragraphs 8–10.

1982 Edition

When sending out his disciples to preach, Jesus said of a city that would reject their message: "Truly I say to you, it will be more endurable for the land of Sodom and Gomorrah on judgment Day than for that city." Matthew 10:15.

By saying this, Jesus showed that at least some of the unrighteous people of ancient Sodom and Gomorrah will be present on earth during judgment day. Although they had been very immoral, we can expect that some of them will be resurrected (Genesis 19:1-26). Jehovah in his mercy will bring them back so they will have an opportunity to learn about his purposes.

1989 Edition

It will truly be a grand privilege to be resurrected on earth during Jehovah's great Judgment Day. However, the Bible indicates that it will be a privilege that not all will enjoy. Consider, for example, the people of ancient Sodom.

Will such terribly wicked persons be resurrected during Judgment Day?

The scriptures indicate that they apparently will not.

…Yes, for their excessive immorality the people of Sodom and of the surrounding cities suffered a destruction from which they will apparently never be resurrected.

Jesus too indicated that the Sodomites may NOT be resurrected.

(6) The "Higher Powers" of Romans 13:1

- Originally the Watchtower Society taught that the "superior authorities" or "higher powers" of Romans 13:1 are earthly governments [*The Time Is At Hand*, 1889, p. 81]

- However, in 1929 this was rejected as a 'false doctrine.' [*Jehovah's Witnesses in the Divine Purpose*, p. 91; *The Truth Shall Make You Free*, p. 312]. The new teaching was that the "higher powers" are God and Christ.

- But decades later the old teaching was adopted again, so that JWs now say Romans 13:1 refers to the earthly governments [WT, 15 May 1980, p. 4; *Man's Salvation ...At Hand*, p. 326]

(7) The Great Pyramid

- The WBTS taught that the Great Pyramid of Giza is "inspired" and "God designed." This was taught for forty-seven years from 1881. [*Thy Kingdom Come* 1891, p. 362; WT, 15 June 1922, p. 187]

- But, in 1928 the Pyramid became "Satan's Bible" and its devotees were charged with having "turned away from Jehovah and his Word." [WT, 15 November 1928, pp. 341, 344].

The second president of the WBTS, Judge Joseph F. Rutherford, did not share Charles Taze Russell's enthusiasm for the Great

Pyramid. He scathingly stated: "If the pyramid is not mentioned in the Bible, then following its teachings is being led by vain philosophy and false science and not following after Christ.... Then Satan put his knowledge in dead stone, which may be called Satan's Bible, and not God's stone witness." [WT, 15 November 1928, pp. 341, 344]

Again: "Let no one today add to his prophecy by saying that a pile of stone in the land of Egypt constitutes God's witness." [*Light II*, 1930, p. 286]

(8) The Title "Abaddon-Apollyon."
- Refers to Satan. [*Studies in the Scriptures*, Vol.7].
- Refers to Jesus Christ. [*Then is Finished the Mystery of God*, p. 232]

Switching from Satan to Jesus Christ is a MASSIVE change.

(9) The "Alpha and Omega" of Revelation.
- Refers to Jehovah God. [*Awake!* 22 August 1978, p. 28]
- Refers to Jesus Christ. [WT, 1 October 1978, p. 15]

This substantial change took place in only two months.

(10) The "Faithful and Discreet Slave" of Matthew 24:45.
- Refers to their founder, Charles Taze Russell. [*Watchtowers* from 1 December 1916 to March 1,1923, p. 68].

- Refers to the "Remnant of Spiritual Israelites" (the supposed remnant of the 144,000 "heavenly class"). [*From Paradise Lost to Paradise Regained*, p. 193]

(11) God's Throne on "Pleiades."

Three articles in the *Awake!* magazine [8 July 1994] deride astrology and star worship. However, each of these articles fails to inform the reader that the Watchtower Society has significantly altered its position with respect to astrology and star worship.

Over Sixty Years

For sixty-two years, (1891 to 1953), the WBTS taught that God resided on the star Alcyone in the Pleiades constellation and that from this star He governed the universe. This belief was propagated in 1891 in Volume 3 of *Studies in the Scriptures* and was allegedly based on passages in the Bible.

The Watchtower also taught that the Great Pyramid of Egypt provided additional proof of God's throne in the Pleiades. [*The Golden Age*, 10 September 1924, pp. 793–794].

In "Reconciliation" the claim is made: "But the greatness in size of other stars or planets is small when compared with the Pleiades in importance, because the Pleiades is the place of the eternal throne of God." [*Reconciliation*, 1928, p. 14]

Doctrine Discarded

The doctrine about Alcyone and Pleiades was discarded in 1953:

"Some attribute striking qualities to these constellations or star groups and on the basis of such they then offer private interpretations of Job 38:31–32 that amaze their hearers... when viewed Scripturally they are completely without foundation." [WT, 15 November 1953, p. 703]

The Bible verses quoted in this 1953 article which the Watchtower derisively claimed had been used by "some" to "amaze their hearers" were in fact the verses used by the Watchtower Society itself to prove that God resided on the star Alcyone. [WT, 15 June 1915, p. 185; *The Golden Age,* 16 May 1928, p. 540]

If this practice does not qualify for the description "deceitful," it would be difficult to imagine what could.

(12) Constellations of the Zodiac.

Given the pattern that has been traced in previous examples of the JWs' doctrinal somersaults, there is a certain inevitability about the fact that:

- the constellations of the Zodiac are presently considered by the WBTS as being of pagan origin [*Insight on the Scriptures*, Volume 2 (1988) p. 1240],
- yet these were regarded in 1914 as being of divine origin with each of the twelve

Zodiacal signs having numerous correspondences with the Bible.

(13) The 1914 Generation

The dramatic alteration in the Watchtower's
teaching concerning "the 1914 generation" is
one of the most noticeable in a process of
changing beliefs.

Playing for Time

The Watchtower Society claimed that
Christ's kingdom had been set up invisibly in
1914, and that all of the prophecies in
Matthew 24–25 would be fulfilled within a
"single generation" (Matthew 24:34); therefore the time of 'the end of the world"
(Matthew 24:3) could be delayed as long as
thirty or forty years. This definition of "generation" promised momentous events during
the 1940's.

- When nothing supernatural had happened by 1945, the Society extended the
  meaning of "generation" to eighty years.
- Two quotations from The Watchtower
  emphasize this substantial change in JW
  teaching:
  (1) ... The expression "this generation"
      was used by Jesus to mark a very
      limited period of time, the life span
      of members of a generation of people
      living during the time that certain
      epoch-making events occurred.
      According to Psalm 90:10, that life -

span could be of seventy years or even of eighty years. Into this comparatively short period of time must be crowded all the things that Jesus prophesied in answer to the request for a "sign when all these things are destined to come to a conclusion." (Mark 13:4)." [WT, 15 December 1967, p. 751]

(2) ...Did not Jesus say that this generation will not pass away until all things are fulfilled? A generation, according to Psalm 90:10, is from seventy to eighty years. The generation that witnessed the end of the Gentile Times in 1914 does not have many more years left." (Luke 21:24, 32–36). [WT, 1 December 1968, p. 715]

• The WBTS did NOT ascribe any special significance to 1994 (1914 plus 80 years); probably because they had already added another major *faux pas* to their "chronic chronological calendar" with some wild speculation about the year 1975, circling that as the latest likely date for Armageddon.

However, by 1994 the "generation" issue was becoming awkward. Time was running out—and the ranks of the Society's special members (the "anointed" 144,000) were dying out.

- Therefore, in 1995, the Watchtower Society decided that "generation" did not mean a physical generation (i.e.eighty years) but meant "age," as in "era." This extended the "end times" indefinitely, and handed the WBTS some much needed "breathing space."

"Date" to State ...

Summary of "The 1914 Generation" Changes in the Awake!

(1) Since the late 1940's *Awake!* magazine had been promising the "sure hope for the establishment of a righteous New World" on page 2 of each issue.

(2) Then in 1964 it added the assurance that this would happen in this generation: "...reflecting sure hope for the establishment of God's righteous new order in this generation."

Elsewhere, the Society defined more precisely what it meant by "this generation": "Jesus was obviously speaking about those who were old enough to witness with understanding what took place when the 'last days' began.... Even if we presume that youngsters fifteen years of age would be perceptive enough to realize the import of what happened in 1914, it would still make the youngest of 'this generation' nearly seventy years old today.... Jesus said that the end of this wicked world would come before that generation passed away in death." [*Awake!* 8 October 1968, p. 13]

(3) In 1975 it was no longer *Awake!* magazine's promise, but it now became the Creator's promise: "...The Creator's promise of a new order of lasting peace and true security within our generation." [*Awake!* 8 January 1975]

(4) In 1982 the Watchtower Society changed the prophecy on page two of each issue of *Awake!* to include the same thought about 1914. It was no longer a vague "our generation" that would see the world's end, but the generation that saw the events of 1914: "...the Creator's promise of a peaceful and secure new order before the generation that saw the events of 1914 C.E. passes away." [*Awake!* 8 January 1982 cf. also WT, 15 May 1984, pp. 6–7]

(5) This prophecy was repeated in each issue of the magazine until 8 January 1987, when *Awake!*'s statement of purpose was moved to page four in a redesigned format. Starting with that issue, the 1914 generation prophecy was dropped entirely, without one word of explanation.

(6) Then it was restored, again without explanation, on page 4 of the 8 March 1988 issue: "...the Creator's promise of a peaceful and secure new world before the generation that saw the events of 1914 passes away." This wording was maintained until 22 October 1995.

The "Old Men" Problem is By Now a Major Headache.

By 1995, however, the generation that saw the events of 1914 had largely passed away. All that remained were a relatively few survivors who were nearly 100 years old. It was obvious the prophecy was under severe strain.

(7) JW leaders in Brooklyn finally replaced this prophecy in the 8 November 1995 edition of *Awake!* by returning to language similar to that used prior to 1964. *Awake!* now declares: "... The Creator's promise of a peaceful and secure new world that is about to replace the present wicked, lawless system of things."

All Reference to "The 1914 Generation" has Been Eliminated.

Suddenly, Jehovah's Witnesses no longer believe in "the Creator's promise of a peaceful and secure new world before the generation that saw the events of 1914 passes away." Yet another date has proven fraudulent.

(14) Vaccinations.

In 1931, the official Watchtower position on vaccinations was: "Vaccination is a direct violation of the Everlasting Covenant that God made with Noah after the flood." ["Golden Age", 4 February 1931, p. 293].

- There was no change by 1935: "As vaccination is a direct injection of animal matter in the blood stream vaccination is a direct violation of the law of Jehovah God." [*Golden Age*, 24 April 1935, p. 465]

- But in a letter dated 15 April 1952 came a significant U-turn on the WBTS policy on vaccinations—the Society finally published the reversal of the vaccination ban. [cf. WT, 15 December 1952, p. 764]

Smallpox was a major problem in the earlier decades of the twentieth century, with a mortality rate of up to 40%. In 1921 there were 100,000 cases in the (civilized) U.S. alone. By 1953 there were none. The vaccination program saved thousands of lives worldwide.

How many died of smallpox (or infected others) as a result of the organization's "rules at the time," is impossible to tell. What is certain is that:

- Jehovah's Witnesses were not permitted to leave or enter countries.
- Jehovah's Witnesses in prison were put in solitary confinement.
- Children were unable to start school without a smallpox vaccination certificate.

There were reports of sympathetic doctors actually scarring children's skin and then issuing a false certificate to enable them to start school. How much better it would have been had the WBTS changed its mind about vaccinations earlier—not merely many unnecessary problems, but many unnecessary deaths, would have been avoided.

(15) The Blood Issue.

The WBTS has long forbidden blood transfusions for Jehovah's Witnesses. The issue is so serious, in fact, that JWs believe a blood transfusion "may result in the immediate and very temporary prolongation of life, but at the cost of eternal life for a dedicated Christian." [*Blood, Medicine, and the Law of God*, p. 55]

Jehovah's Witness parents are expected not only to prevent their children from undergoing a blood transfusion [Ibid., p. 54], but also even to prevent family pets from receiving blood. [WT, 15 February 1964, p. 127]

In order to prevent their being administered blood transfusions while unconscious, each Witness is required to carry a card that states:

"I direct that no blood transfusions be administered to me, even though others deem such necessary to preserve my life or health. I will accept non-blood expanders. This is in accord with my rights as a patient and my beliefs as one of Jehovah's Witnesses. I hereby release the doctors and hospital of any damages attributed to my refusal. This document is valid even if I am unconscious, and it is binding upon my heirs or legal representatives."

The Watchtower Society forbids blood transfusions because the procedure allegedly constitutes eating blood, which is forbidden in the Bible in Genesis 9:4 and Acts 15:28–29. They contend that receiving blood intravenously constitutes eating, just as people can receive food intravenously. [*Jehovah's Witnesses and the Question of Blood*, p. 18]

Rollercoaster Ride

However, the position of the WBTS on the issue of blood transfusions has not remained constant, but has resembled a "roller coaster ride."

- 1909: Acts 15:13–15 (including prohibition on blood) is not considered as a law for Christians. [WT Reprints 1909, p. 4374]
- 1945: Blood transfusions denounced as pagan and God dishonoring. [WT, 1 July 1945, pp. 198–201]
- 1961: Taking a blood transfusion was grounds for "disfellowshipping," while donating organs (eyes) for transplant is up to your own conscience. [WT, 15 January 1961, pp. 63–64; WT, 1 August 1961, p. 480]
- 1963: Any fraction of blood considered as a nutrient is not to be used in medical treatment. [WT, 15 February 1963, p. 124; *Awake!* 22 February 1975, p. 30]
- 1967: Organ transplants are a form of cannibalism and to be shunned. [WT, 15 November 1967, pp. 702–704]
- 1977: Blood transfusions are organ transplants: "... Many a person might decline blood simply because it is essentially an

organ transplant that at best is only partially compatible with his own blood."
[*Jehovah's Witnesses And The Question Of Blood*, 1977, p. 41]

- 1978: Ban on certain blood fractions lifted for hemophiliacs. [WT, 15 June 1978, p. 30]
- 1980: Organ transplants are a matter of conscience, decided by the individual. [WT, 15 March 1980, p. 31, cf. 1977 ruling.]
- 1984: Accepting a bone marrow transplant is up to your conscience. However, the manner in which the WBTS argue the issue would lead a correctly trained conscience to say no. [WT, 15 May 1984, p. 31]

The Victims

It is a sad fact to ponder that a large number of Jehovah's Witnesses, including many children, have died due to their loyalty to the Watchtower Society's brutal and unscriptural position on blood transfusions.

The 22 May 1994, issue of *Awake!* featured the stories of five children who died after refusing blood transfusions. These stories, emotive in both tone and rhetoric, depict children who inspired respect and acceptance for the Society as they "happily sacrificed their lives" to uphold the Watchtower's regulations. The reality of the situation is, however, much more grim.

In a particularly horrifying example of how seriously Jehovah's Witnesses take the Society's prohibition, Paul Blizard recounts his experience when his daughter needed a transfusion. After Blizard accepted a court order requiring that his daughter receive a transfusion, an elder said, "I hope your daughter gets hepatitis from that blood." [*Witnesses of Jehovah*, p. 197]

Blizard, his wife, and even their daughter were then shunned by their congregation for not smuggling the girl out of the hospital to avoid the transfusion.

Another Twist? . . . Dramatic News From Bulgaria

On 9 March 1998, the European Commission of Human Rights accepted a settlement between the government of Bulgaria and the Christian Association of Jehovah's Witnesses in which the Bulgarian government, in exchange for a significant concession from the Witnesses, agreed to recognize the Witnesses as an official religious organization and to provide civilian service for conscientious objectors to military service. [Information Note No.148; http://194.250.50.201 /eng/E276INFO.148.html]

The compromise made by the Society is far more noteworthy. The Watchtower Society agreed, on the subject of blood transfusions, that "members should have free choice in the matter for themselves and their children, without any control or sanction on the part of the association." [Ibid.]

A press release distributed in 1997 by the Commission clearly explains how the Commission and the Bulgarians understood the Watchtower's stated position: "In respect of the refusal of blood transfusion, the applicant association (i.e., the Jehovah's Witnesses) submits that there are no religious sanctions for a Jehovah's Witness who chooses to accept blood transfusion and that, therefore, the fact that the religious doctrine of Jehovah's Witnesses is against blood transfusion cannot amount to a threat to 'public health'." [Press Communique Issued by the Secretary to the European Commission of Human Rights, Application No. 28626/95; http://www.dhcommhr.coe.fr/eng/28626CP.E. html]

Worldwide Liberty?

This concession seems to be a remarkable reversal of Watchtower doctrine. It raises the question: will the Watchtower Society now extend this new liberty for Jehovah's Witnesses to receive blood transfusions to all of its adherents worldwide, not merely those who reside in Bulgaria?

Another possibility is: was the Society disingenuous in its agreement with the Bulgarian government?

The Watchtower Position

A definite clue to the Watchtower's true position may be found in a press release distributed by the Society on April 27, 1998. The only information about the Bulgarian agreement to allow transfusions is this statement:

"The agreement also includes an acknowledgment that each individual has the freedom to choose the type of medical treatment he receives."

This vague statement, while not openly contradicting the agreement, also contains no indication of the historic compromise to which the Society agreed by ostensibly allowing blood transfusions.

The view of most informed observers is: despite their agreement to allow JWs to receive blood transfusions in Bulgaria, in reality the Society has no intention of honoring this agreement. It will be happy to publicly trumpet its (new) "It's-up-to-the-individual's-own-conscience line, while continuing with its usual practice of levying religious sanctions against Witnesses who receive blood transfusions, forcing the Witnesses to decide between possible death or "excommunication or disfellowshipping."

"Quote" to **Note**
Some Good Home-Grown Advice

I close this chapter with a student word straight from another Jehovah's Witness manual. Once again, it is some exceptionally good "homegrown" advice...

"How would you feel if proof is given that what you believe is wrong?

For example, say that you were in a car, traveling for the first time to a certain place. You have a road map, but you have not taken the time to check it carefully. Someone has told you the road to take. You trust him, sincerely believing that the way he has directed you is correct, but suppose it is not? What if someone points out the error? What if he, by referring to your own map, shows that you are on the wrong road? Would pride or stubbornness prevent you from admitting that you are on the wrong road?

Well, then, if you learn from an examination of your Bible that you are traveling a wrong religious road, be willing to change. Avoid the broad road to destruction; get on the narrow road to life." [*You Can Live Forever In Paradise On Earth*, pp. 32–33].

A more complete example of "a wrong religious road," or "strong delusion" (2 Thessalonians 2:11, Matthew 24:11) than what we have in the Watchtower Bible And Tract Society would be difficult to find. If only the governing body (and each individual member) of the Watchtower Society would follow their own guidance, countless more would stream out of the suffocating grip of this man-centered organization and into the true liberty of a child of God through Jesus Christ our Lord.

Conclusion

Speaking to Jehovah's Witnesses is quite a challenge. They are specifically trained not to act positively to anything you say, so if you show them a Scripture that challenges their belief, or a photocopy of an article in their own magazine *The Watchtower* that shakes their faith in their organization, they will not overtly acknowledge that.

Remembering this fact will assist us greatly in any discussion with them. Do not expect them to draw breath and admit, "You've got a good point there. I didn't know that. That really shakes me." Even though that may be exactly what they are feeling inside (and many ex-Jehovah's Witnesses have testified to the penetration of their defenses and mind-set that they have experienced when speaking to an Evangelical Christian), they are trained not to react like that. How they react when they lay their heads on the pillow at night may be quite another thing.

Ex-Jehovah's Witness, David Reed, recalling one occasion when a Christian pointed out to him that Jehovah and Jesus were both called "The Alpha and the Omega—the first and the last" [cf. Question 14, p. 28] even in his own JW "Bible", says that while he did not flinch when that was pointed out, but argued with the Christian... "When I got home, I panicked; I opened my Watchtowers; I was researching; I saw the Watchtower's answer to it, and I thought, 'Well, that takes care of it,' ... but still when I laid my head down on my pillow at night, I thought, 'It still bothers me; I wonder if he was right?'"

Reed also remembered how one Christian had shared his personal testimony with him, outlining the change in his life and speaking of his living relationship with God. That bothered him. He knew he had a relationship with an organization; he studied about God in the *Watchtower* magazine, but he had no personal, living relationship with God, and he knew, from the New Testament, that the people in the first century church *did* have a living relationship with God.

Years later, when the Holy Spirit began to draw him to Christ, he testified that none of the words earnest Christians had spoken to him were wasted.

The Jehovah's Witnesses can be saved ... and many thousands have been. Many books have been written and articles posted on the internet by ex-Jehovah's Witnesses—those whose eyes God has graciously opened to see the bondage of the Watchtower and the glory of His gospel.

If we, as Christians, are to be a link in the chain of our Lord's great providential purpose that sees some Jehovah's Witness reclaimed from the error of his way and regenerated by the power of God the Holy Ghost, patience is required, as is prayer and love.

Paul's lament over the spiritual darkness that had fallen upon the hearts and minds of his own countrymen should strike a chord with us as we consider the plight of the Jehovah's Witnesses (Romans 10:1–4, 8, 14):

"Brethren, my heart's desire and prayer to God for Israel is, that they might be saved. For I bear them record that they have a zeal of God, but not according to knowledge. For they being ignorant of God's righteousness, and going about to establish their own right-eousness, have not submitted themselves unto the righteousness of God. For Christ is the end of the law for righteousness to every one that believeth.

How then shall they call on him in whom they have not believed? and how shall they believe in him of whom they have not heard? and how shall they hear without a preacher? ... The word is nigh thee, even in thy mouth, and in thy heart: that is, the word of faith, which we preach."

That is the scale of the challenge that faces us. I pray we will rise to it, and that this little book will have some role to play in setting forth "the word of faith, which we preach."

HOW TO USE THIS BOOK EFFECTIVELY

How to use this Book Effectively

You will quickly discover that this book does NOT read like a novel with an "I-couldn't-leave-it-down-until-I'd-finished-it" quality. Certainly some of the teachings of the JWs are novel and incredible and pretty ridiculous. Were they not so serious, they would prompt many a smile.

The primary purpose of this book is to put information into the hands of God's people that will help them to answer, and witness to, the misguided JW on their doorstep. As such it is a reference work; the good thing about it is, you will be able to award it a permanent place in your library and keep returning to it. Believe me, given the dedication of the JWs, you will need it.

It is not likely that one would memorize ALL of the questions (plus the Bible references and facts) contained in this book for the next time a Jehovah's Witness calls at your door. However, there are a number of key questions that are worth committing to memory. These are listed below.

Source of Authority – Question No. 3

Even if light does become brighter, it never contradicts former light. [Note: This will allow you to discuss the "Doctrinal Somersaults" the Jehovah's Witnesses have engaged]

The Trinity –*Question No. 4 Part III*

How can the Watchtower Society construe belief in the Trinity as a deception of the devil when each of these three persons is designated "God" [Greek, Θεος] in Scripture (e.g. The Father, John 6:27; the Son, Hebrews 1:8; the Holy Spirit, Acts 5:3–4)?

NOTE: Jehovah's Witnesses will object that the word "trinity,"- which expresses the Biblical teaching of three Persons (tri) in one God (unity), is not found in the Bible; therefore it cannot be true.

Simply point out to them that the terms "millennium," "theocracy," and "rapture" are not found in Scripture either. Will they stop believing their teaching on these subjects because of the absence of these words in Scripture?

The Person of Christ –*Question No. 14 (p. 28)*

Since there can be only one who is 'the first and the last" and both Jehovah and Jesus are called this in Scripture, Jesus must be God.

The Holy Spirit –*Question No. 33*

Acts 5:3–4 clearly identify the Holy Spirit as God.

NOTE: Jehovah's Witnesses not only deny the Deity of the Holy Spirit, but also His personality. A quick and effective line of reasoning to show that the Bible teaches the Personality of the Holy Spirit is to follow a widely accepted definition of what a person is,

(1) A person has a mind. The Holy Spirit has a mind: 1 Corinthians 2:10–11 describes Him as having thoughts and possessing knowledge.

(2) A person has emotions. The Holy Spirit is described as having emotions. He can be hurt (Isaiah 63:10) and be grieved (Ephesians 4:30).

(3) A person has a will. In 1 Corinthians 12:11, the Holy Spirit is said to give gifts to each person "just as he wills."

Salvation –*Question No. 35*

Ephesians 2:8–9 and Titus 3:5 are most explicit that salvation is by faith alone in Jesus Christ alone—and NOT OF WORKS.

Death and Eternity –*Question No. 48*

How can "anyone" be "tormented ... forever and ever" if the wicked are supposed to be annihilated?

The End Times –*Question No. 52*

When Watchtower doctrine insists that ONLY 144,000 are "born of God," why does 1 John 5:1 insist that ALL Christians are "born of God"?

"Everyone believing that Jesus is the Christ has been born from God..."?

Doctrinal Somersaults –*Question to Note*

Why does Watchtower teaching on the men of Sodom and Gomorrah change so drastically from 1982 and 1983: will they be resurrected or not? (cf. extended note on this subject on pp. 96–97).

NOTE: Remember the proven technique: ASK QUESTIONS.

SUGGESTED READING AND FURTHER INFORMATION

Suggested Reading

Apocalypse Delayed, The Story of Jehovah's Witnesses (University of Toronto Press, 1985) by M. James Penton

Awake to the Watchtower (Reachout Trust, 1993) by Doug Harris and Bill Browning

Dangerous Delusions (A.R. Mowbray & Co., 1961) by Kenneth N. Ross

Dictionary of Theological Terms (Ambassador-Emerald International, 2002) by Alan Cairns, www.emeraldhouse.com

Do Jehovah's Witnesses Contradict the Bible? (Bob Jones University Press, 1975) by Stewart Custer

How to Answer a Jehovah's Witness (Bethany House Publishers, 1980) by Robert A. Morey

How to Get Jehovah's Witnesses to Listen (Comments from the Friends, 1998) by David A. Reed, www.cftf.com

Jehovah's Witnesses and Judge Rutherford's Books (Central Bible Truth Depot) by Al. Pollock